THE EPIC OF FLIGHT

Memo to the Reader:

The Aeronauts, like every book in the Epic of Flight series,
is being translated into half a dozen languages for distribution
around the world. To interest so broad an audience, we knew we
had to create a truly international book. And that, I am glad to
say, is just the kind of challenge our unique network of researchers,
correspondents and string correspondents thrives on. Their search
for the photographs, art and artifacts that you will find in
The Aeronauts became a worldwide treasure hunt.

The quest began close to home: While a team of four researchers
was dispatched to investigate such domestic resources as the Richard
Gimbel Aeronautical Collection at the United States Air Force Academy,
and the Eleutherian Mills Historical Library in Delaware, Picture
Editor Richard Kenin took the subway from his house in Washington,
D.C., to the Library of Congress. There, dressed for what he knew
would be a dirty job, he sought out one of the oldest surviving
collections of aeronautica, assembled in the 19th Century by the
French balloonists Gaston and Albert Tissandier.

On the dim and dusty lowest-deck-but-one of the great library,
Kenin foraged through engravings, lithographs, watercolors, posters,
photographs and printed ephemera--all stowed in large flat boxes
stacked on narrowly spaced racks, and mostly uncatalogued. Each
night for several nights he emerged blinking and sneezing with
some new find for the book.

In France, our Paris correspondents, Maria Vincenza Aloisi and
Josephine du Brusle, scouted in the Musée Carnavalet, the Musée de l'Air
and a number of provincial museums--including American Malcolm Forbes's
Chateau de Balleroy in Normandy--to unearth valuable images.

From England, our history consultant, Charles Gibbs-Smith (who
is Sherlock Holmes reincarnate when such game is afoot), directed
us to Rome and Countess Maria Fede Caproni. At her family palace,
the Countess presides over a private museum--begun by her famous
father, the Italian aviation pioneer Gianni Caproni, and little
known outside aviation circles. It turned out to include a trove

TIME
LIFE
BOOKS

TIME-LIFE BOOKS INC., ALEXANDRIA, VIRGINIA 22314

of balloon images and artifacts. The museum has no staff, but
once persuaded by our Rome correspondent, Ann Natanson, the Countess
became our ally in research.

It was the Countess who went, on our behalf, to Münster, Germany,
to attend the most important exhibition in this century of lighter-
than-air history, mounted by the Westfälisches Landesmuseum. She
returned with study photographs and a catalogue that guided our
Bonn correspondent, Elisabeth Kraemer, toward items in private
collections rarely seen before. (The catalogue itself became precious
overnight; not only are no more available, but there were reports
that copies of it were disappearing in the German mails.)

Our search spread: to Tokyo, where Time-Life Books Asia Editor
Nakanori Tashiro discovered that Japan's 19th Century introduction
to Western ways included demonstrations by American balloonists,
which led in turn to the creation--and preservation--of charming
wood-block balloon triptychs by Japanese engravers; to Warsaw,
where string correspondent Bogdan Turek found a photograph of the
1938 Gordon Bennett race, won by Polish aeronauts in the last year
their nation was free; to London, where string correspondent Karin
Pearce concluded that an exquisite balloon-shaped dressing-table
ornament at the Science Museum--some said it came from the boudoir
of Marie Antoinette--felt suspiciously like plastic. Experts were
summoned; the globe, they determined, was made of 19th Century
celluloid--too late for Marie Antoinette, but eligible at least for
our essay on fine balloon artifacts.

And back to Washington where Picture Editor Kenin, having
extracted himself from the Tissandier collection, was in frustrated
pursuit of Mathew Brady's photograph of the American Civil War
balloonist Thaddeus Lowe. When it was published, half a century
after the War, the photograph showed a balloon all right, but no
balloonist. Lowe immediately wrote that he could see his arm in the
picture, but the rest of him had been cropped out. Every printable
version Kenin could lay hands on suffered from the same cropping.

Finally the Library of Congress made a print for us directly
from Brady's original glass negative--and there, for the first time
in a century, is Mr. Lowe. You will find him on pages 84-85, one
of 131 illustrations gathered from nine nations, in The Aeronauts.

                    Cordially,

                    Tom Flaherty

                    Thomas H. Flaherty Jr.
                    Series Editor
                    The Epic of Flight

THE AERONAUTS

THE AERONAUTS

by Donald Dale Jackson

AND THE EDITORS OF TIME-LIFE BOOKS

TIME-LIFE BOOKS, ALEXANDRIA, VIRGINIA

Time-Life Books Inc.
is a wholly owned subsidiary of

TIME INCORPORATED

FOUNDER: Henry R. Luce 1898-1967

Editor-in-Chief: Henry Anatole Grunwald
Chairman of the Board: Andrew Heiskell
President: James R. Shepley
Editorial Director: Ralph Graves
Vice Chairman: Arthur Temple

TIME-LIFE BOOKS INC.

MANAGING EDITOR: Jerry Korn
Executive Editor: David Maness
Assistant Managing Editors: Dale M. Brown (planning),
George Constable, George G. Daniels (acting), Martin Mann,
John Paul Porter
Art Director: Tom Suzuki
Chief of Research: David L. Harrison
Director of Photography: Robert G. Mason
Senior Text Editor: Diana Hirsh
Assistant Art Director: Arnold C. Holeywell
Assistant Chief of Research: Carolyn L. Sackett
Assistant Director of Photography: Dolores A. Littles

CHAIRMAN: Joan D. Manley
President: John D. McSweeney
Executive Vice Presidents: Carl G. Jaeger,
John Steven Maxwell, David J. Walsh
Vice Presidents: George Artandi (comptroller);
Stephen L. Bair (legal counsel); Peter G. Barnes;
Nicholas Benton (public relations); John L. Canova;
Beatrice T. Dobie (personnel); Carol Flaumenhaft
(consumer affairs); Nicholas J. C. Ingleton (Asia);
James L. Mercer (Europe/South Pacific); Herbert Sorkin
(production); Paul R. Stewart (marketing)

THE EPIC OF FLIGHT

Editorial Staff for *The Aeronauts*
Editor: Thomas H. Flaherty Jr.
Designer: Donald S. Komai
Chief Researcher: Pat S. Good
Picture Editor: Richard Kenin
Text Editors: Russell B. Adams Jr.,
Bobbie Conlan, Lee Hassig
Staff Writers: Malachy Duffy,
C. Tyler Mathisen, Sterling Seagrave
Researchers: Judith W. Shanks (principal), Diane Bohrer,
Patti H. Cass, Cathy Gregory, Sara Mark,
Carol Forsyth Mickey, Blaine M. Reilly
Assistant Designer: Van W. Carney
Editorial Assistant: Kathy Wicks

Editorial Production
Production Editor: Douglas B. Graham
Operations Manager: Gennaro C. Esposito, Gordon E. Buck
(assistant)
Assistant Production Editor: Feliciano Madrid
Quality Control: Robert L. Young (director), James J. Cox
(assistant), Daniel J. McSweeney, Michael G. Wight
(associates)
Art Coordinator: Anne B. Landry
Copy Staff: Susan B. Galloway (chief), Elizabeth Graham,
Diane Ullius Jarrett, Cynthia Kleinfeld, Brian Miller,
Celia Beattie
Picture Department: Nan Cromwell Scott

Correspondents: Elisabeth Kraemer (Bonn); Margot
Hapgood, Dorothy Bacon, Lesley Coleman (London); Susan
Jonas, Lucy T. Voulgaris (New York); Maria Vincenza Aloisi,
Josephine du Brusle (Paris); Ann Natanson (Rome). Valuable
assistance was provided by Nakanori Tashiro, Asia Editor,
Tokyo. The editors also wish to thank Martha Mader,
Helga Kohl (Bonn); Karin Pearce (London); Carolyn T.
Chubet, Miriam Hsia, Christina Lieberman (New York);
M. T. Hirschkoff (Paris); Mimi Murphy (Rome).

THE AUTHOR

Donald Dale Jackson, a former staff writer for *Life,* has written two volumes for Time-Life Books in The American Wilderness series: *Sagebrush Country* and, with Peter Wood, *The Sierra Madre.* He spent a year at Harvard University as a Nieman Fellow. Among his other books are *Judges,* a history of the United States judicial system, and *Gold Dust,* a narrative history of the gold rush. *The Aeronauts* is the culmination of a long-standing personal interest in ballooning.

THE CONSULTANT for The Aeronauts

Captain Roger Pineau, U.S.N.R. (Ret.), was assistant to Samuel Eliot Morison in the preparation of the 15-volume *History of U.S. Naval Operations in World War II.* His scenario for a movie adaptation of *The Divine Wind* is based on a book about Kamikaze pilots in World War II that he edited and translated from the Japanese. His interest in ballooning began when he was asked to research and coordinate the aeronautical exhibition at the National Air and Space Museum.

THE CONSULTANTS for The Epic of Flight

Melvin B. Zisfein, the principal consultant, is Deputy Director of the National Air and Space Museum, Washington. He received degrees in aeronautical engineering from the Massachusetts Institute of Technology and has contributed to many scientific, technological and historical publications. He is an Associate Fellow of the American Institute of Aeronautics and Astronautics.

Charles Harvard Gibbs-Smith, Research Fellow at the Science Museum, London, and a Keeper-Emeritus of the Victoria and Albert Museum, London, has written or edited some 20 articles and numerous articles on aeronautical history. In 1978 he served as the first Lindbergh Professor of Aerospace History at the National Air and Space Museum, Smithsonian Institution, Washington.

Dr. Hidemasa Kimura, honorary professor at Nippon University, Tokyo, is the author of numerous books on the history of aviation and is a widely known authority on aeronautical engineering and aircraft design. One plane that he designed established a world distance record in 1938.

For information about any Time-Life book, please write:
Reader Information
Time-Life Books
541 North Fairbanks Court
Chicago, Illinois 60611

Library of Congress Cataloguing in Publication Data
Jackson, Donald Dale, 1935-
    The aeronauts.
    (The Epic of flight; 4)
    Bibliography: p.
    Includes index.
    1. Balloons—History. I. Time-Life Books.
II. Title. III. Series: Epic of flight; 4.
TL616.J33   629.13'09   79-26804
ISBN 0-8094-3268-4
ISBN 0-8094-3267-6 lib. bdg.

CONTENTS

A global profusion of airborne spheres

The concept of a sky filled with balloons has intrigued people of every age and nationality for almost two centuries, ever since men embarked on their first lighter-than-air voyages in 1783.

From the outset, balloons have been put to uses as varied as the colors with which they brighten the air. Artists, as the 19th Century lithograph at right suggests, have found the balloon's image an irresistible vehicle for satire. Generations of sportsmen, professional showmen, explorers and scientists have made them the means to their particular ends. Even warriors have commandeered these most peaceful of creations for service as spy platforms, as carriers of bombs and as vehicles of escape and communication for cities under siege.

Though overtaken in the 20th Century by the advent of faster and more tractable airborne vehicles, balloons have remained, as a British aeronaut wrote, "the one mode of travel that has never grown up." This aura of innocence, coupled always with the imminence of danger that accompanies intrusion into an uncertain element, has kept the enchantment of ballooning intact. Today, venturesome men and women by the hundreds ride aloft in these Gargantuan rafts of the air. Filling the sky *(pages 168-169)* to an extent their forebears scarcely dreamed of, they share the sense of liberation that prompted an early balloonist to declare, "I feel as though I had left behind me all the cares and passions that molest mankind."

Balloons, as national symbols, crowd the sky in this Italian cartoon from the 1870s. The artist lampoons no fewer than 23 countries, among them imperialist Great Britain (top center); expansionist Russia, whose balloon (right of center) is already the largest; Prussia (top right), whose gondola is a spiked helmet; and the United States (top left), whose lighthearted citizens are lifted by the balloons of several states, bound together.

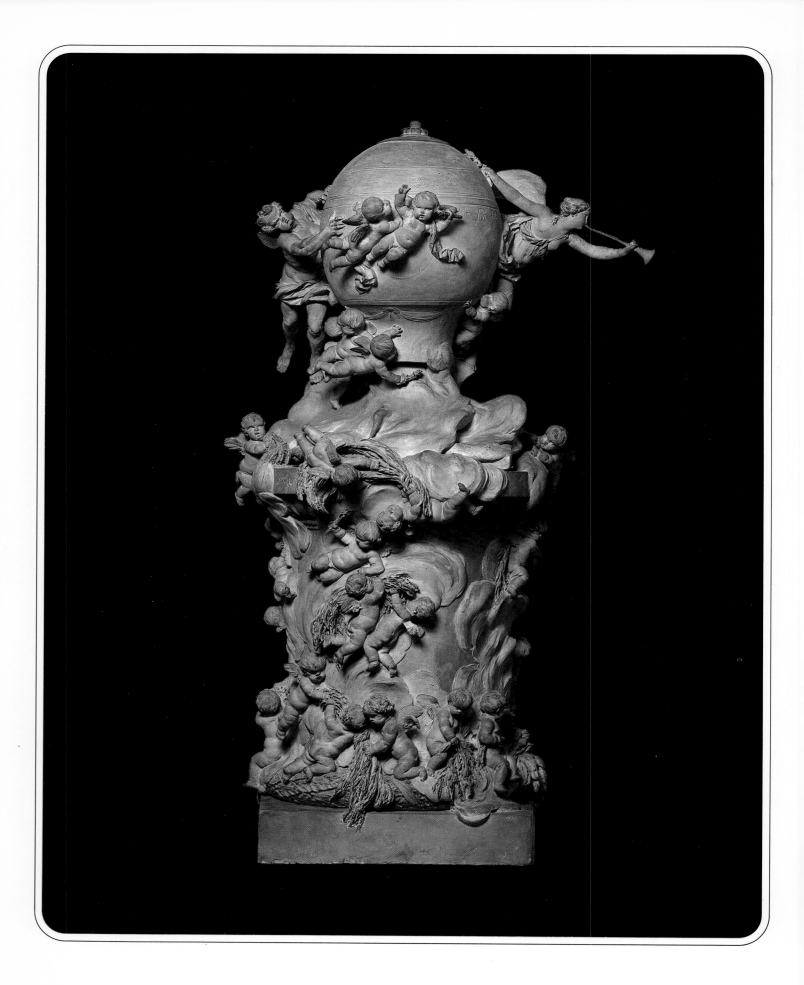

1
"Show us the way to the skies"

On a fine December afternoon in 1783, the Duke of Villeroi watched skeptically from his apartment window overlooking the Tuileries gardens in Paris as preparations were completed for the ascent of a manned balloon. Although he had heard reports of other such experiments by his countrymen in recent weeks, the Duke, like many in the crowd that had gathered outside, had little faith that the device would leave the ground. A few minutes later, however, the balloon did take off, and the aging nobleman, watching it rise above the trees, fell to his knees as one who had witnessed a miracle. "Yes, it is certain!" he prophesied of the men who now waved from the car suspended beneath the colorful silken globe. "They will find out the secret of avoiding death."

The balloonists had not, of course, discovered a way to elude death—in fact, some of them would meet it all too soon. But they *had* found a way of expanding the experience of living, of liberating themselves at least temporarily from the shackles of gravity to float unhindered in a new and fascinating dimension.

The sight of their fellow mortals soaring toward the heavens that afternoon so astonished the hundreds of thousands of earth-bound Parisians who caught at least a glimpse of the free-floating balloon that, like the Duke, they would remember 1783 as an *annus mirabilis*—a year of wonders.

From a ballooning standpoint the year of wonders had in fact begun just six months before, and not in Paris but in the South of France, where two brothers had devised a way to capture hot air from a fire in a large bag made of paper and cloth. Joseph Michel and Jacques Étienne Montgolfier were scions of a family that had manufactured paper in the provinces for four centuries. By 1782, when Joseph began his first tentative experiments with balloons, the prosperous business at Annonay, south of Lyons, had been designated a "royal manufactory," supplier of paper to the Kings of France. The income that accompanied this honor gave Joseph, then 42, and Étienne, 37, the affluence to tinker at whatever they wished.

Joseph Montgolfier turned his attention to balloons—although the reason is enshrined more in fable than in fact. One story has it that the principle of lighter-than-air flight occurred to him when he saw his wife's chemise being wafted upward when it was hung before a fire. Another attributes the original inspiration to a simple paper cone

Winged infants, a trumpeting goddess of fame, and Aeolus, god of the winds, hail the advent of the hot-air balloon in this rococo statuette. The French sculptor Claude Michel Clodion submitted the terra-cotta work in 1784 as a model for a monument to lighter-than-air flight proposed—but never built—by Louis XVI.

used to package sugar; when tossed onto a fire the cone rose up the chimney without igniting.

Actually, the physical basis for such phenomena was well enough known in Montgolfier's time. The Greek mathematician Archimedes had expounded it nearly 2,000 years before in his treatise, "On Floating Bodies." Archimedes wrote that an object immersed in a fluid is buoyed up by a force equal to the weight it displaces. By the same reasoning, a balloon or other vehicle containing a substance lighter than air would rise until its weight matched that of the atmosphere around it.

Over the years, various men tried to apply Archimedes' principle to flight. None succeeded, usually for the lack of a lifting element. But Joseph Montgolfier, a well-educated and practical man, had read about the discovery in 1766 of a gas that weighed just one fourteenth as much as air. Henry Cavendish, the brilliant English recluse who was responsible for this discovery, recognized the explosive nature of the gas; he called it "phlogiston," the 18th Century name for the element that was supposed to make all combustible substances burn. In 1783 the gas acquired its modern name, hydrogen, though most laymen knew it simply as "inflammable air."

In his first experiments, Joseph Montgolfier filled small paper globes with hydrogen and sent them aloft, duplicating some earlier efforts by Tiberius Cavallo, an Italian-born experimenter then living in England. Cavallo had had little success with his tests and Montgolfier at first fared no better. His balloons rose only a few feet, then descended precipitously as the gas escaped through the fibers of the paper. Unlike Cavallo, however, Joseph Montgolfier persisted. Finding silk to be similarly pervious to hydrogen, he abandoned his efforts with the gas and cast about for some other substance that was lighter than air but not as difficult to contain as hydrogen.

Cavallo, who became an eloquent historian of early ballooning, wrote later that Montgolfier, having observed "the natural ascension of the smoke and the clouds in the atmosphere," decided to "imitate these bodies, or to enclose a cloud in a bag, and let the latter be lifted up by the buoyancy of the former."

Trapping clouds was obviously impractical, but Joseph—whether or not inspired by watching his wife's chemise take flight over a fire—thought that perhaps smoke could be made to work as a lifting agent. What he did not understand was that it was the *heat* in smoke that made air expand, and therefore rise; he thought the smoke itself was the substance he was looking for, and indeed was convinced that the fouler the smoke smelled, the more lifting power it possessed. Accordingly, he burned a mixture of damp straw and chopped wool that gave off a promisingly unpleasant aroma.

After a successful indoor experiment with a small balloon, Joseph showed his invention to his brother Étienne, who at once caught his enthusiasm for the lighter-than-air project. Together they built a larger balloon, inflated it with smoke, and watched in rapt fascination as it rose

JOSEPH MICHEL MONTGOLFIER

JACQUES ÉTIENNE MONTGOLFIER

This stained historic print shows the first public ascension of the Montgolfiers' unmanned hot-air balloon, from a field near Annonay, France, on June 4, 1783.

gradually to a height of some 70 feet before the smoke cooled (the brothers no doubt thought that it had merely escaped) and the balloon floated back to earth.

Through early 1783 the Montgolfiers refined their creation, trying various combinations of cloth and paper in the balloon envelopes, enlarging the dimensions and watching their unmanned balloons soar ever higher, eventually to 1,000 feet. In June they constructed their biggest one yet—a paper liner inside a strong linen skin that measured 110 feet in circumference and had a volume of 22,000 cubic feet—and invited the local people to view its ascent from a field not far from the Annonay town square. The result was all that the Montgolfiers could have hoped for: The hot smoke from a large fire transformed the ponderous folds of paper and fabric into a great bouncing globe restrained by a perspiring crew of eight men who clung to the square wooden frame at its base. At Joseph Montgolfier's signal, the men released the balloon and it climbed away from the awed spectators to an altitude estimated at 6,000 feet. There it floated elegantly for some 10 minutes before dropping lightly to earth a mile and a half downwind.

Acclaim for the Montgolfiers was instantaneous. News of their stunning success traveled rapidly from the provinces to Paris, the intellectual and cultural—as well as political—capital of France, and set off a sunburst of invention that soon launched the science of aerostatics, the study of how to make a balloon rise, descend or float at a constant altitude. Almost at once a new vocabulary sprouted. Ballooning became known as aerostation. The balloons themselves were called aerostats, and those who went up in them (often called philosophers, the 18th Century word for physicists) were hailed as aeronauts.

The prestigious Academy of Sciences in Paris accepted a proposal by a young physicist, Professor Jacques Alexandre César Charles, that he duplicate—and thereby validate—the Montgolfiers' achievement. Charles had been misled, however, by a report of the Montgolfiers' flight that had been published in the *Journal de Paris;* he believed that the brothers had inflated their balloon with hydrogen. This misconception set Charles on a road that would lead to the creation of an entirely different kind of aerostat—and to a good-natured, and highly productive, rivalry with the Montgolfiers.

By August, Charles, then 37 years old, was ready to introduce Paris to the air age, and the city could hardly wait. Indeed, hundreds of Parisians had helped to finance the building of the balloon by paying one crown apiece for the privilege of a close-up view of its anticipated takeoff from a special enclosure. "Among all our circles of friends," wrote the philosopher Friedrich Melchior Grimm, "at all our meals, in the ante-chambers of our lovely women, as in the academic schools, all one hears is talk of experiments, atmospheric air, inflammable gas, flying cars, journeys in the sky."

That Charles had made such rapid progress was due in large measure to the work of Jean and Noël Robert, Parisian craftsmen who had invented a rubber coating for silk that made it less permeable to hydrogen, thus solving the problem that had defeated Joseph Montgolfier in his experiments with the elusive gas. In a few weeks Charles and the brothers Robert, working in their shop in the Place des Victoires, produced a spherical aerostat with a diameter of 13 feet and a volume of 943 cubic feet, a dwarf compared to the Montgolfiers' giant, but—because of the hydrogen it contained—able to lift more weight per cubic foot. They intended to fill the balloon at the bottom through a hoselike neck of fabric containing a valve that would be closed after inflation. But the gassing operation, which began on August 23 in a small walled yard adjoining the Roberts' shop, turned out to be much more difficult than expected.

In 1783, the best way to produce hydrogen in quantity was through the action of dilute sulfuric acid on iron filings. But the apparatus the inventors had built to contain the reaction leaked so freely that it had to be rebuilt. Then the gas being piped into the balloon grew so hot from the chemical reaction between the acid solution and iron that it threatened to ignite the fabric, which had to be cooled with water. As

How hydrogen was made

Hydrogen was far lighter and—though inherently volatile—relatively safer than hot air, which required an open fire. Nevertheless it had two drawbacks as a lifting agent for early balloons: It was expensive to produce and the process was tediously time-consuming.

Originally, hydrogen was produced by the reaction of dilute sulfuric acid and such metals as iron and zinc. In arrangements like the one at right, sealed casks filled with dilute sulfuric acid and iron filings were interconnected with pipes made of tin. As the acid-iron mixture bubbled away, the hydrogen thus produced was forced through the pipes into a main feeder line to the balloon.

To stabilize the balloon and make it easier for the hydrogen to enter it, the envelope was strung between two masts by a cable that ran through a ring at its top. Once the envelope was filled—a process that might take several hours or several days—the cable helped to restrain the balloon until lift-off.

By the 1790s a less expensive method—isolating the hydrogen content of water by passing steam continuously over hot iron in a tube—was in use as a way of generating the large amounts of hydrogen needed by a balloon. And in 1821 coal gas, often available at city mains, was introduced as a cheaper and less explosive alternate to hydrogen.

An elaborate apparatus used for producing hydrogen is shown in this 1790 drawing. The small pails at the top of the casks served as funnels for pouring the iron filings and dilute sulfuric acid into the casks. The small balloon attached to a cask at the far end, when inflated, indicated the presence of hydrogen. The cross section at center shows the gas-release valve, located at the top of the main balloon.

a result, water vapor in the hydrogen condensed in the balloon and began to fill it. Moreover, the water contained a mild acid that ate away at the rubber coating inside, causing leaks. Meanwhile public excitement had mounted to such a pitch that the first demonstration could not be delayed much longer.

By the fourth day the exhausted crew had finally piped enough gas into the sphere for a tethered flight to an altitude of 100 feet. Rising above the roofs of Paris, the aerostat drew a throng whose very size threatened to ruin the balloon. Before the scheduled launch, the inventors decided to move the balloon to the more spacious grounds of the Champ-de-Mars, where a century later the Eiffel Tower would rise. The balloon was hauled down, lashed by ropes to a wagon and—late at night, to avoid attracting a crowd—was convoyed along the nearly deserted avenues of Paris. With its escort of mounted guardsmen and torchbearers—the latter a palpable hazard near the hydrogen—the balloon was the central figure in a bizarre parade. "The cab drivers on the road were so astonished," wrote Barthélemy Faujas de Saint-Fond, another one of ballooning's early historians, "that they were impelled to stop their carriages, and to kneel humbly, hat in hand, whilst the procession was passing."

All through the following day, August 27, the crowd assembled. Those who had paid their money—including the 77-year-old scientist-philosopher Benjamin Franklin, at the time America's diplomatic representative to France—were permitted to enter the enclosure where the balloon underwent final preparations; others overflowed the park onto nearby streets, rooftops and quays along the River Seine. At 5 p.m. a single cannon shot signaled that the balloon had been released.

"A little rain had wet it, so that it shone," Franklin wrote. "It diminished in apparent magnitude as it rose, till it enter'd the clouds, when it seem'd to me scarce bigger than an orange, and soon after became invisible, the clouds concealing it." At that point a spectator who was standing near Franklin turned to him and asked the disparaging question that would pursue balloons throughout their subsequent history: "What good is it?" To which Franklin replied reasonably, "What good is a newborn baby?"

At 5:45 p.m., the infant aerostat, appropriately named the *Globe,* descended on Gonesse, 15 miles northeast of Paris. It might have stayed up longer but, because there was no way to relieve the increasing pressure of the hydrogen as the balloon ascended into lighter air, the cloth tore, letting out much of the gas.

The first men to see the downed balloon, its twisted form writhing on the ground as the hydrogen escaped, concluded that it was a monster that had been dispatched by some vengeful neighbor. Terrified, they hurled stones at it as other peasants came running. A Paris journal described what happened next: "The creature, shaking and bounding, dodged the first blows. Finally, however, it received a mortal wound, and collapsed with a long sigh. Then a shout of victory arose; and a new

JACQUES CHARLES, FATHER OF THE GAS BALLOON

valor reanimated the victors." A man cautiously approached the balloon and thrust a knife into its body, which released a final gasp of sulfurous gas, driving back its assailants. When at last the ogre was subdued, the men of Gonesse tied it to a horse and then dragged it ignominiously to the village.

Parisians, unlike their rural countrymen, hailed this spectacular new phenomenon. Historian Cavallo reported that a balloon craze began to blossom in Paris. Miniature gas-filled replicas, made from the rubbery animal membrane known as goldbeater's skin (because it was used by the craftsmen who pounded gold into gold leaf to protect the fragile material from direct blows of the hammer), soon were being sold in shops along the boulevards. To reassure the rest of France that balloons were harmless, and to prevent a recurrence of the debacle at Gonesse, the government issued a proclamation throughout the land announcing that further experiments were planned with even larger balloons. The bulletin assured the populace that a balloon "is only a machine, made of taffetas, that will someday prove serviceable to the wants of society."

The fearful peasants of Gonesse jab Professor Charles's balloon to death in this 18th Century French engraving.

The *Journal de Paris* asked that anyone finding a balloon report its whereabouts and condition to the newspaper.

Both entreaties were written with the knowledge that the Montgolfier brothers had been summoned to Versailles to demonstrate their hot-air machine for King Louis XVI and his court. Indeed, Étienne Montgolfier had arrived in Paris to begin work on a new balloon in time to witness the flight of Jacques Charles's *Globe.* Étienne's presence in the capital—Joseph, less outgoing than his brother, preferred to seclude himself in Annonay and continue his experiments—added the ginger of competition. By September 14—just 18 days after the ascent of the *Globe*—Étienne had prepared a spectacular balloon with, as Cavallo noted, "a very odd shape. Its middle part was prismatic; its top was a pyramid; and its lowest part constituted a truncated cone."

To help inflate his seven-story giant, Étienne built a platform several feet above the ground. A hole in the platform would permit smoke from a fire below to enter the balloon, which was held erect over the hole between two masts. One advantage of a hot-air balloon over a hydrogen balloon became apparent when Étienne readied his elaborately painted creation for a tethered test flight, to which members of the Academy of Sciences had been invited. In contrast to the four days necessary to fill the hydrogen balloon, the "montgolfier"—as hot-air balloons had come to be called—was inflated and straining at its ropes after a mere 10 minutes over a smoky fire. Then, just as the crew released the linen-and-paper balloon to test its lifting power, a sudden, gusty rainstorm caused it to pull violently against its mooring lines. The balloon ripped apart, a total loss.

The performance for the King was only five days away. Étienne hurried to construct a new balloon—this time in the shape of a simple elongated sphere. His tireless workmen cut bolts of cotton cloth into long strips, stitched them together to make a globe and lined the inside with paper. In just four days, a balloon 57 feet high and 41 feet in diameter had been sewed, painted and tested.

Montgolfier reached Versailles with the balloon at 8 a.m. on September 19. Standing next to a platform that had been built to help in filling the balloon, he explained to King Louis how the device would lift its cargo. Speculation had it that a man would go up in the balloon, but Étienne had decided to experiment first with lesser animals: A sheep, a cock and a duck, suspended in a wicker cage, were selected as the first creatures to fly in a man-made device.

At 1 p.m., Montgolfier lit a fire that was fed by old shoes and decomposing meat, as well as wet straw, to produce what he considered to be the best smoke possible for the flight. Most of the acrid emanations billowed up a canvas chimney into the balloon, but enough escaped to drive Étienne's royal hosts to a less malodorous vantage point. "In four minutes," wrote Étienne to his brother Joseph at Annonay, "the machine was filled. Everybody let go at once, and the machine rose majestically. Just a moment after lift-off, along came a gust of wind that laid it

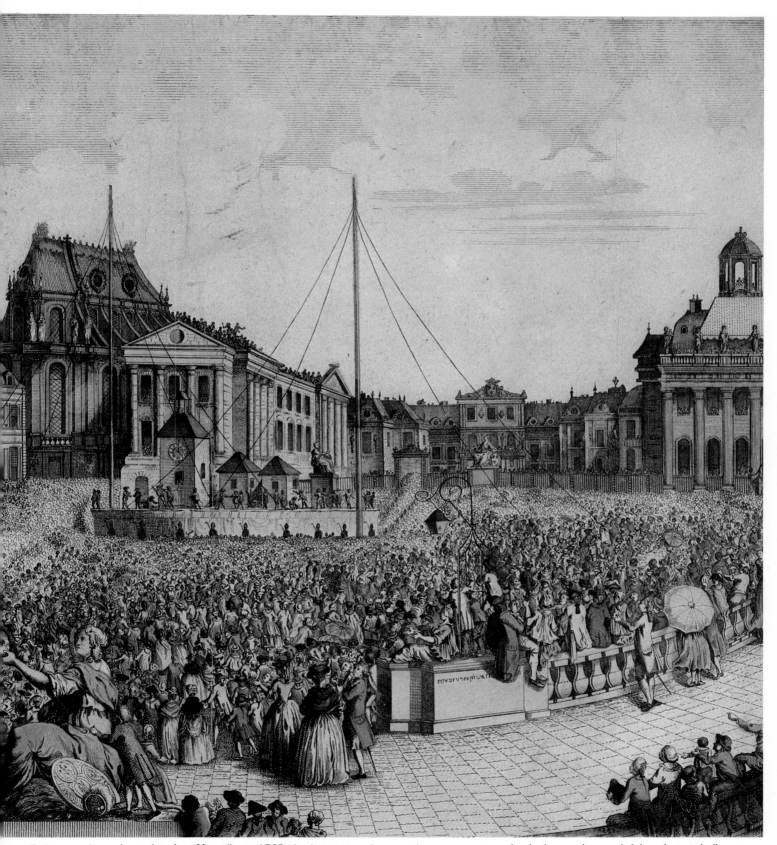

Before royalty and a multitude at Versailles in 1783, the first air travelers—a sheep, a rooster and a duck—are borne aloft by a hot-air balloon.

on its side. At that moment I feared failure." But the balloon recovered and continued to rise, bearing away its live cargo on a light breeze. The royal audience cheered.

Two astronomers calculated the balloon's altitude to be 1,700 feet before it began to sink toward a forest two miles away. Several of the spectators hurried to the landing site, where they found that the cage had been jarred open by a branch encountered during the descent and that the animals were loose. The sheep and the duck appeared none the worse for their adventure, but the cock seemed to have injured one of his wings during the flight. The animal's injury prompted much headshaking over man's future safety in the skies—until several witnesses came forward to testify that the sheep had kicked the rooster before the balloon had even left the ground.

The flight pleased the King, but when Étienne Montgolfier announced his intention of constructing a man-carrying balloon, His Royal Highness insisted that the passengers be criminals, who would be offered a pardon if they survived the trip. A zealous aristocrat named François Pilatre de Rozier, at 26 years of age one of the youngest members of the Academy, objected strenuously to the King's order. Pilatre de Rozier was incensed that convicted felons were to be offered the glory of being the first men into the air. Instead he offered himself for the experiment.

The young nobleman, who was best known for having founded a scientific museum in Paris, was also something of a daredevil. He delighted and alarmed visitors to his museum by inhaling hydrogen and then igniting it as he exhaled. He also possessed courage and coolness in adversity—qualities that would prove important in a balloonist—and a gift for swaying important men.

Pilatre de Rozier persuaded François Laurent, the Marquis d'Arlandes, to use his influence with one of Queen Marie Antoinette's ladies in waiting to help secure the King's assent to sending an honorable Frenchman, rather than a criminal, aloft. D'Arlandes succeeded, but he demanded compensation for his assistance: He would accompany Pilatre de Rozier on the flight.

The balloon Étienne had begun building was the most ambitious yet. The major additions were a wicker passenger gallery that was built around the base of the balloon like a circular balcony, and a fire basket suspended by chains beneath the aperture at the bottom of the globe, so that the aeronauts could keep the balloon filled with smoke and thus remain airborne longer. Also placed on board were forks to pitch bundled straw onto the fire and buckets of water with sponges to save the balloon if it began to smolder. Pilatre de Rozier made his first captive, or tethered, ascent to a height of 84 feet in this balloon on October 15 in Paris; he was so excited on landing that he violated one of the as yet unwritten rules of ballooning by jumping out of the gallery before the balloon was secured; the sphere, freed of his weight, promptly bobbed back up to the end of its tether.

François Pilatre de Rozier, pilot of the first manned balloon, is shown conducting an experiment that earned him incidental fame: igniting exhaled hydrogen gas.

The Marquis d'Arlandes courageously joined Pilatre de Rozier on the first manned flight. Later, in the French Revolution, he was cashiered for cowardice.

In a contemporary colored etching, Étienne Montgolfier's balloon tugs on its mooring lines just moments before being released from the Bois de Boulogne, near Paris, on November 21, 1783. The world's first aeronauts, d'Arlandes and Pilatre de Rozier, are saluting the crowd from opposite sides of the balloon's circular gallery.

Pilatre de Rozier was unperturbed. "The intrepid adventurer," wrote Cavallo, "assured his friends and the multitude, which had gazed on him with admiration, with wonder, and with fear, that he had not experienced the least inconvenience: no giddiness, no incommoding motion, no shock whatsoever." Four days later Pilatre de Rozier went up again, still tethered, first to 210 feet, then to 262 feet, and finally twice to 320 feet, accompanied the last time by the Marquis d'Arlandes.

Tests complete, the balloon was taken out of Paris early on November 20 to the garden of the Crown Prince's palace in the nearby Bois de Boulogne. The next morning, though the flight had not been publicized, a crowd of Parisians gathered for the spectacle. It was a gray and gusty day and on the final tethered test the wind caught the balloon and ripped it in several places before it could be tied down. As hastily assembled workmen began to repair the damage, the crowd became increasingly restive at the delay. After two hours, however, everything at last seemed ready; even the wind had subsided. Étienne Montgolfier pronounced himself satisfied. Flames reached toward the restless globe from the wire-mesh fire basket, and the great blue-and-gold sphere inflated to its full majesty—seven stories high and two thirds that broad. Pilatre de Rozier and d'Arlandes stationed themselves on opposite sides of the gallery, to keep it in balance.

The crowd fell silent; the crew on the ground let go the ropes attached to the gallery and the balloon rose gently, wonderfully, into the air. It was 1:54 p.m. Slowly it drifted higher, heading across the park and the city on a soft northwesterly breeze. At an elevation of about 280 feet the world's first aeronauts doffed their hats to the throng below. "I was surprised at the silence and the absence of movement among the spectators," d'Arlandes wrote afterward. The onlookers were apparently too astonished to speak.

D'Arlandes himself was so entranced by the sight of the city diminishing beneath him that he let his attention stray from the task at hand—keeping the fire going. Pilatre de Rozier abruptly intruded on his reverie: "You are doing nothing," he cried, "and the balloon is scarcely rising a fathom." D'Arlandes hurriedly tossed a bundle of straw onto the fire and observed with satisfaction that the toy-sized buildings below him grew noticeably smaller.

The spectators on the ground, craning their necks to follow the path of the balloon, were equally enchanted. "Soon the aerial navigators were lost from view," wrote the correspondent for the *Journal de Paris,* "but the machine, floating on the horizon and displaying a most beautiful shape, climbed to at least 3,000 feet, at which height it was still visible; it crossed the Seine and was borne to a position where it could be seen by all Paris."

But on board the balloon matters had taken a distressing turn. Several minutes into the flight, d'Arlandes noticed with some alarm that the fire was burning holes, some "of considerable size," in the balloon fabric and threatening the cords that connected the gallery to the balloon. Indeed, two of the lines had already parted with an alarming snap. Grabbing the sponge and bucket of water brought along for just such an emergency, d'Arlandes worked quickly to extinguish the fires in the fabric, thereby averting a catastrophe.

After d'Arlandes's fire-fighting stint, the aeronauts saw that they were dropping uncomfortably close to the rooftops of Paris. Calmly they threw more straw on the brazier and rose out of danger. A short time later they allowed the fire to subside and, 25 minutes after takeoff, they plopped gently down between two millhouses, slightly more than five miles from where they had started.

This first landing by a manned balloon illustrated a timeless peculiarity of that conveyance: For all its sublime and majestic bearing in the air, on the ground it is little more than a billowing heap of unruly cloth. D'Arlandes, climbing over the wicker railing, felt the rapidly cooling balloon sag onto his head. He looked for Pilatre de Rozier, and, he

A gold medallion, struck at the order of King Louis XVI, commemorates the remarkable aeronautic feats of 1783 —the first ascensions of both hot-air (left) and hydrogen-filled balloons.

Professor Charles's balloon is brought back to Paris in a triumphal procession on the 2nd of December, 1783, the day after its historic 27-mile flight from the Tuileries. The partially deflated balloon "was escorted by several persons of distinction," said one report, "to the cheers of the people."

reported, "saw him in his shirt sleeves creeping out from under the mass of canvas that had fallen over him."

Considering the disasters that might have befallen it, this first flight was an unqualified success—and a sensation. The historian Cavallo tried to re-create the wonder of the event. "Imagine a man elevated to such a height," he wrote, "by means altogether new, viewing one of the greatest towns existing, crowded with spectators expressing, in every possible manner, their amazement, and their anxiety. Reflect on the prospect, the encomiums, and the consequences; then see if your mind remains in a state of quiet indifference."

During the days that followed the ascent of the manned montgolfier, Professor Charles and the Robert brothers worked at modifying their own balloon for a manned flight. In doing so they gave the gas-filled balloon all its major features, elements that have remained fundamentally unchanged through two centuries. The neck of the new device, instead of having a valve, would be left open so that hydrogen could escape from the balloon as it ascended, thus relieving pressure that might otherwise burst the taut fabric. Charles did add a valve at the top of the balloon; by pulling on a cord that ran from the valve down

Fascinated crowds watch Francesco Zambeccari's golden balloon rise over Venice in this contemporary painting.

Stormy adventures of an Italian aeronaut

The father of experimental ballooning in England was not British, but Italian. Born in Bologna, Count Francesco Zambeccari had been serving as an officer in the Spanish navy when, after a brush with the Inquisition, he fled to England in 1782. The British had never been much interested in French ballooning, but Zambeccari, inspired by the Montgolfiers, plunged into his own experiments—and was soon rewarded.

With no fanfare, on November 4, 1783, he released a small unmanned hydrogen balloon from a London rooftop. People rushed out to watch in astonishment as it drifted over the city. Zambeccari worked feverishly to build a more impressive balloon for a public launch. He made a 10-foot globe of silk, varnished with oil and veneered with gilt, and on November 25 he sent it aloft before a large assemblage at the Moorfields Artillery Ground. The balloon stayed up more than two hours before landing intact at Graffam, 48 miles away.

But Zambeccari's days of success in England were numbered. In early 1784 he concocted a grandiose scheme to build a 50-foot man-carrying balloon, but the plan failed for lack of money. The next year, when one of his balloons failed to lift off, the spectators rioted. Zambeccari, angry and broke, left England for his native Italy, where his misadventures continued to overshadow his successes; an 1803 flight ended with a dunking in the Adriatic *(below)*.

The Count went up for the last time in September 1812. As his balloon descended to treetop level, it caught fire. Zambeccari leaped to escape the flames and was killed by the fall.

"We were dragged and beaten at the mercy of the waves," wrote Zambeccari of his forced landing in the Adriatic with two fellow balloonists in October of 1803. The engraving below describes their rescue by fishermen, after four frightening hours at sea.

through the center of the balloon and out the neck, an aeronaut could slow his climb or return to earth. To rise again, Charles prescribed a supply of sand as ballast that could be poured overboard to lighten the craft. A wicker car was suspended from a cord net that covered the upper half of the balloon and thus distributed the weight of the car equally over the top of the sphere.

Just 10 days after d'Arlandes and Pilatre de Rozier concluded their pioneering free flight in the montgolfier, Charles was ready to outdo them in his new red-and-white-striped aerostat, again financed by public contribution. Charles's balloon, 26 feet in diameter, was transported to the Tuileries already inflated for the takeoff.

"All Paris was out," a delighted Benjamin Franklin wrote. "Never before was a philosophical experiment so magnificently attended." Or so enthusiastically debated: Proponents of the gas balloons argued that their greater ability to lift (because hydrogen is much less dense than hot air) and the absence of a fire on board the balloon itself made them better and safer than the montgolfiers, even though the hot-air balloons could be inflated more quickly.

But such arguments had no place among the inventors themselves. When everything was ready for takeoff, Charles approached Étienne Montgolfier, who was in the audience. "It is for you, monsieur," said Charles graciously, "to show us the way to the skies," and handed him an emerald-colored five-foot-wide balloon to test the wind. Together the two men watched the little globe float off to the northeast. Then, under the gaze of the skeptical Duke of Villeroi and the waiting crowd, Charles and his copilot Noël Robert climbed on board the car, which had been provisioned against the cold with blankets, furs and champagne. They unloaded 19 pounds of sand and, at the report of a cannon, sailed soundlessly aloft.

Once more, the audience was dumbstruck. Franklin studied the balloon through a pocket telescope, watching as it ascended to 200 feet, where "the brave adventurers held out and wav'd a little white pennant, on both sides of their car, to salute the spectators." At this sign that the men were safe, the assemblage exploded in thunderous applause.

Charles was equally moved. "Nothing," he wrote, "will ever equal that moment of joyous excitement which filled my whole being when I felt myself flying away from the earth. It was not mere pleasure; it was perfect bliss." The balloon seemed to hang pinned to the sky as Charles and Robert, keeping an eye on the barometer that they had brought with them, vented hydrogen or tossed blankets and clothing overboard (one of the blankets landed on the dome of the Church of the Assumption) to maintain a constant altitude, as Charles had assured his friends that he could. After nearly an hour, a cannon boomed in the distance— this was the signal that they were beyond sight of Paris now and free of the necessity to fly at a specific height. "We gave ourselves up," wrote Charles, "to the views which the immense stretch of country beneath us presented." After another hour they touched down on a field 27 miles from the Tuileries, but the exhilarated Charles was not yet sated. He ascended once again, after Robert climbed out of the car, to become the world's first solo aeronaut.

With the loss of Robert's weight the balloon shot up like a rocket. "I passed in 10 minutes from the temperature of spring to that of winter," Charles wrote. "The cold was keen and dry but not insupportable. I examined all my sensations calmly; I could hear myself live, so to speak." According to barometer readings, which the scientist Charles could translate into altitude, the balloon peaked at nearly 10,000 feet, high enough for the sun, which had set for those on the ground, to beam on him once again. "I was the only creature on the horizon in sunshine—all the rest of nature was in shade." A few minutes later he was delighted to witness his second sunset of the day.

But all of a sudden the professor cut his ascension short because he was stricken by sharp pains in his right ear and jaw, probably caused by the change in air pressure. He released some gas through the bal-

Angered by the delay of a promised ascent in Paris in 1784, a crowd reacts riotously in this period engraving. The hot-air balloon had ignited during inflation, and the spectators, who had paid to see the event, fed the fire with their chairs and ladders.

loon's valve, and as he returned to earth he controlled the speed of his descent by carefully shedding ballast until he glided to a moonlit landing on a plowed field.

After Charles's tour de force, a madness for balloons swept France. Shops bulged with balloon-shaped hats, fans, clocks and bird cages. Waistcoats and sword handles, tobacco cases and candy boxes were ornamented with balloon designs; medallions depicting the gaily decorated montgolfiers were especially popular. The fad soon surfaced on the stage in such productions as *The Balloon, or Physicsmania.* In the salons, according to one historian, "people danced the contra-dance of Gonesse," named for the village where the first hydrogen balloon had landed. One French writer speculated that the new creation would be the nemesis of customs-tax collectors, "who henceforth will never be able to prevent the passage of contraband." Caricaturists endowed the female anatomy with balloon-shaped protuberances, and Benjamin Franklin wrote to a friend: "We think of nothing here at present but of flying. The balloons engross all attention."

In the beginning this fascination with ballooning was confined primarily to France. Across the Channel the British, who were almost reflexively skeptical of anything French, were initially hostile to balloons. Though Franklin had tweaked the president of Britain's Royal Society by suggesting that, in the matter of aerostation, "your philosophy seems too bashful," the Society responded to an order by King George III for an inquiry into balloons with the pronouncement that "no good whatever" could result from such experiments. A London newspaper called upon the people of England to "laugh this new folly out of practice as soon as possible." Not surprisingly, when the first balloon flew over Britain—it was unmanned and went aloft in November of 1783—it was not sent up by an Englishman, but by an Italian who was living in London, Count Francesco Zambeccari.

In France, however, doubters by now were a minority, and the science progressed. When word reached Lyons of Étienne Montgolfier's successful demonstration for the King at Versailles, the Academy of Sciences at Lyons prevailed upon Joseph Montgolfier in nearby Annonay to duplicate the experiment that had so pleased the King. Using money collected from the local citizenry, Joseph designed a massive balloon 126 feet high and 100 feet in diameter. At its base was a gallery large enough to hold six men.

Test inflations of the leviathan began early in 1784 but were hampered first by freezing, rainy weather, which stiffened the cloth-and-paper balloon, and later by fire, which partially consumed the envelope when Montgolfier tried to thaw it. The balloon was finally ready for demonstration in Lyons on January 19 before a crowd of 100,000. On board were Joseph Montgolfier (making his first and only flight), Pilatre de Rozier and four insistent noblemen. At Pilatre de Rozier's sensible suggestion that the crew of the fire-weakened balloon be limited to

Carried away by the manifold possibilities of ballooning, Swiss artist B. A. Dunker in 1784 produced the grand, carefully keyed— and wildly impractical—engraving at left. For a journey to the Far East, the whimsical balloon was depicted carrying a church and hospital (K); an outhouse (U); sleeping facilities for passengers (P); a caterer's quarters and café (X); and separate, cagelike housing for prostitutes (R).

three, the noblemen had brandished their swords and dared anyone to evict them. To add to the load in the gallery, an impetuous youth who had helped to build the balloon leaped on board at the last minute, just as it began to lift off.

The ground crew had forgotten to release two of the mooring ropes, and the balloon dragged ominously toward the crowd, creating a moment of panic before the ropes were cut and the balloon finally lurched skyward. Minutes later, a sickening rip heralded the appearance of a four-foot tear in the top of the balloon. Within seconds hot air began to escape faster than the fire tenders could replace it. As the hole grew ever larger, the balloon fell rapidly from an altitude of 3,000 feet; it slammed heavily to earth after only 18 minutes aloft. The first spectators to reach the landing site saw nothing but flames and a vast, heaving canvas, but their dismay turned to relief as first one of the shaken passengers, then another and then the rest emerged from beneath the fabric. Only two of them had been injured: One sword-wielding count broke a tooth; another bruised his leg. That evening the seven aeronauts attended the opera in Lyons where they were recognized as they entered their box. The show was halted mid-note and the audience gave the balloonists a standing ovation.

The ascent at Lyons proved to be the last such venture by the Montgolfiers. In the years that followed they continued to write about aeronautics, but they devoted most of their energies to other interests. Joseph invented a hydraulic pump, while Étienne took an influential post in provincial government. Professor Charles too, for all his rhapsodic delight in ballooning and his obvious skill as a balloonist, never flew again. The earache he had endured on his climb to 10,000 feet evidently had been enough for him. However, these pioneers had done their work admirably, planting the seeds that would yield a bountiful and lasting harvest.

By now, ballooning was spreading beyond France. Near Milan, Italy, in February 1784, Chevalier Paulo Andreani ascended in a montgolfier, accompanied by Augustin and Charles Gerli, who had built the balloon. Similar experiments took place in Austria and Scotland. The inaugural flight in the New World, in June of the same year, was a tethered ascent by a 13-year-old boy named Edward Warren in Bladensburg, Maryland. Young Warren volunteered to go aloft in a hot-air balloon built by lawyer Peter Carnes after the aerostat proved insufficiently buoyant to carry Carnes himself. A month later Carnes attempted a free flight in Philadelphia, but his craft ascended too slowly and collided with a wall, dumping him to earth from a height of 12 feet.

Yet the question that Benjamin Franklin had so neatly deflected the previous summer—What good is a balloon?—remained unanswered. The obstacle to the practical application of aerostation was the problem of control, a technical difficulty that many savants of the 18th Century believed would give way before a concentrated assault by scientific minds and methods. It was in this spirit that the Academy of

The distressing tale of an inflated balloonist

The public's early enthusiasm for ballooning was by no means unanimous. While much of society grew delirious with balloon fever—Benjamin Franklin, for example, was invited to a friend's house in Paris "for tea and balloons"—others looked upon the newfangled invention with a decidedly jaundiced eye.

Among the skeptics were many cartoonists and caricaturists of the day. Almost immediately after the first ascensions, artists of humor began taking aim at balloons and those who flew in them. Balloonists were shown as vainglorious fools, their vessels as glorified soap bubbles, and their rabid supporters as riffraff or worse. (In one British cartoon published in 1783 the central figure in a group of human balloon watchers was portrayed as an ape.)

The satirical scene below illustrated the popular tale of an ailing French gentleman who was addicted to ballooning. Through a mistake, he received from his physician an injection of "inflammable air" intended for his balloon—and turned into a balloon himself. To the horror of his family, he was carried out of his bedchamber by the gas and was soon lost from sight.

In a farcical watercolor entitled The Day's Folly, a gas-inflated Parisian becomes lighter than air.

Lyons, early in 1784, offered a 50-livre prize for the best essay on the subject of the "safest, least expensive and most effectual means of directing air balloons at pleasure."

The resulting quest for lateral navigation focused on oars pulled by the aeronauts and on rudder-like flaps attached to the balloon itself. In April two citizens of Dijon ascended in a gas balloon equipped with such appurtenances, but the experiment was nearly undone when one oar was lost and a rudder on the same side was damaged. The balloonists nonetheless convinced themselves that their diligent rowing with the remaining oar had had "some effect" on their direction. Two months later the Robert brothers, who had invented the rubber coating that made hydrogen-filled balloons possible, ventured aloft with the Duke of Chartres in an elongated aerostat that they proposed to steer by means of a rudder. Two parasols mounted on the car were supposed to propel them forward or backward when opened or closed. Both ideas were dead ends: A balloon offers more resistance to the air than an oar does; oars (or parasols) could only stir the air. Balloonists also experimented with sails—which were equally useless, since a balloon is itself a kind of sail and travels with the wind.

Nevertheless, by the end of 1784 there was plenty of evidence that balloons could travel high and far, if not in a chosen direction. Pilatre de Rozier ascended in a montgolfier to an altitude of 11,700 feet over Versailles in June. Three months later the achievement of his craft was eclipsed by that of a hydrogen balloon that soared across France for an astonishing 150 miles before landing its pilot in the middle of a garden party at a nobleman's château.

It became increasingly clear after this flight that hydrogen-filled balloons offered many advantages over the hot-air variety. Improvements in the production of the gas reduced the montgolfier's main attraction—that it could be quickly inflated. Moreover, hot-air balloons appeared more dangerous because of the fire they had to carry, even though balloonists knew hydrogen to be highly explosive. Many cloth-and-paper hot-air balloons burned up on landing, and others returned to earth scorched. Almost all of the montgolfiers had to be junked after only one flight, while a hydrogen balloon could be folded up to be flown at another time.

It was for such reasons that aeronaut Jean Pierre Blanchard chose a hydrogen-filled aerostat for the exploit that would make him famous. Blanchard was born into a poor family in the Norman village of Les Andelys; destined to grow no bigger than a jockey, he learned as a youth that he would have to scramble for what he got in life. He was a mechanically gifted young man who in another era might have tinkered up a horseless carriage or a wireless; as it was, when he was 16 years old he built a four-wheeled forerunner of the bicycle that he called a veloci-pede. In his twenties he turned his talents to the problems of flight and produced a contraption he called a Flying Ship in which a set of pedals and two hand levers were connected to four large flapping wings. Blan-

The framed drawing above bears a profile of aeronaut Jean Pierre Blanchard, who with Dr. Jeffries made the first Channel crossing. Their exploit is depicted at bottom.

Wearing gloves and a leopard-skin cap against the cold, Dr. John Jeffries is shown reading a barometer on the first aerial crossing of the English Channel, in 1785.

chard wisely abandoned the project—the device never would have flown—and in 1783, as soon as he heard of the Montgolfiers' success, turned enthusiastically to ballooning.

Lacking both the influence and the affluence of such men as Pilatre de Rozier, Charles and the Montgolfiers, Blanchard buttressed his mechanical skills with a genius for self-promotion; he became ballooning's first "professional." By 1785 he had also become the world's best-known, most widely traveled and most maligned balloonist, a hero-for-hire who would court sponsors, advertise for an audience, float aloft with the receipts and profit once again by selling his account of the flight for publication. Indisputably courageous, the bantam Blanchard was also humorless, jealous and mean-spirited, an egotist with an aversion to sharing the limelight.

On his early ascents Blanchard attached wings to the car of his balloon, in the belief that he would thus be able to steer it. He had so much confidence in these useless wings that he predicted the destination of his first flight, only to be borne in the opposite direction by an uncooperative breeze.

Blanchard made three more flights before the mockery of his critical countrymen drove him to decamp for England. There he soon acquired a sponsor in Dr. John Jeffries, a Boston-born physician whose Tory sympathies had impelled him to flee the Colonies during the Revolutionary War. Ascending before the Prince of Wales and other dignitaries on November 30, 1784, Blanchard, Jeffries and the latter's pet dog endured a chilly one-and-a-half-hour ride during which Jeffries collected samples of the air high above the ground for study by the Royal Society. They descended in the Kent countryside and almost immediately began planning a more ambitious project—the first aerial passage of the English Channel.

The Channel was an irresistible challenge. Logically the honor of conquering it belonged to France, the nation that had brought ballooning to its current status, but England, despite the scornful attitude of much of its Establishment, had stirred itself to action: James Sadler, the first important British-born aeronaut, had made his initial flight in October of 1784 on board a hot-air balloon. Sadler also had his eye on the Channel, and in December he began preparations for a flight to France. Meanwhile Pilatre de Rozier, inspired by a promised reward from the French government, readied a balloon for an attempt from the opposite shore, into the teeth of the prevailing westerly winds. Blanchard, in his attempt, would fly under dual colors: As he had been born a Frenchman and was sponsored by Britons, his gondola would display the flags of both countries. By late December Blanchard and Jeffries were in Dover, awaiting clear weather.

Jeffries had agreed to pay the £700 expenses of the flight in return for the privilege of accompanying Blanchard across the Channel. But Blanchard schemed to the last to reserve all the glory for himself. He even hired a tailor to line his vest with lead, so that at the weighing-in on the morning of the takeoff he could use the extra weight to argue that Jeffries must stay behind. (The tailor mistakenly delivered the vest to Jeffries and the ruse was exposed.) Despite Blanchard's scheming, on January 7, 1785, Jeffries took his place in the gondola alongside Blanchard, amid food, brandy, flags, self-promoting leaflets, bags of ballast, extraneous oars, cork jackets (to be used as life preservers) and a small propeller that Blanchard planned to turn by hand to help move the balloon. The balloon rose from atop the white cliffs at 1 p.m. and drifted out over the Strait of Dover.

Riding a gentle westerly, the aeronauts floated slowly toward the Continent. Jeffries succumbed to the grandeur of the flight: "We began to have a most enchanting prospect of the distant country back of Dover," he wrote, "enjoying in our view a great many towns and villages." But the balloon soon began to lose altitude, probably because of leaks in the envelope or because of the lower temperature over the Channel, which caused the gas in the balloon to contract. By the time they were two thirds of the way to France they had jettisoned the last of their ballast to check their descent; still they were not high enough for safety. When they began to descend below the crest of the bluffs that marked the French Coast, they fell back on a balloonist's last, desperate resort: They dumped everything overboard.

"My noble little captain gave orders, and set the example," Jeffries wrote, "by beginning to outstrip our aerial car, first of our silk and finery." Over the side went the oars, the propeller, and two anchors, "after which my little hero stripped and threw away his coat. On this I was compelled to follow his example. He next cast away his trousers. We put on our cork jackets and were, God knows how, as merry as grigs to think how we should splatter in the water." But the lightened gondola now rose again, and at 3 p.m., "almost benumbed with cold," they were thrilled to see the French shore beneath them.

A half hour later, the balloon again began to descend, this time threatening the aeronauts with a crash landing in a forest about 12 miles inland. This time they threw out their cork life jackets. When that had little effect, Jeffries suggested an imaginative expedient: "From the recollection that we had drank much at breakfast and not having had any evacuation," he reported delicately, "an extra quantity had been secreted by the kidneys, which we might now avail ourselves of by discharging." They did so, filling two containers and dropping them over the side. A couple of pounds lighter, the balloon cleared the edge of the woods and Blanchard landed it in a small clearing. We were "almost as naked as the trees," wrote Jeffries, with "not an inch of cord or rope left, no anchor or anything to help us, nor a being within several miles." The only objects that remained in the car were Jeffries' thermometer and barometer, a bottle of brandy and a packet of letters; history's first airmail had arrived in France.

Blanchard pulled on the valve line, venting enough gas to collapse the balloon. Then the scantily clad aeronauts settled back to await

Blanchard and Jeffries leave the cliffs of Dover behind en route to France in this oil painting. Their boat-shaped gondola was equipped with oars for steering, but they proved useless. The stern sail was the product of the artist's imagination.

rescue—and fame. Their triumph was complete: Sadler had been forced to scrap his mission because fresh varnish stuck his folded balloon together and it could not be inflated when it arrived in Dover; Pilatre de Rozier, poised on the French Coast, had been thwarted by contrary winds. Once discovered, Blanchard and Jeffries were borne into Calais on "an elegant chariot" like the conquerors they were. Soon afterward they were summoned into the presence of King Louis, who rewarded his countryman Blanchard with 12,000 livres and a pension of 1,200 livres per year. Jeffries received no reward but contented himself with the admiration of "hundreds of the first ladies and gentlemen in Paris."

Blanchard's success only intensified the frustration of his rival Pilatre de Rozier. After graciously adding his congratulations to the plaudits showered on Blanchard in Paris, Pilatre de Rozier returned to his long weather watch on the French side of the Channel, under a royal command to make the first east-west crossing. Bad weather forced him to scuttle two scheduled lift-offs in January and a third in April.

The balloon designed for his flight was an unlikely hybrid of the Montgolfier and Charles creations. A hydrogen balloon was to supply

the lift, while a cylindrical, fire-fed hot-air balloon suspended beneath it was to serve as adjustable ballast by having its fire stoked or banked. Thus the balloon could descend without venting hydrogen and reascend with a hotter flame. The valve line, instead of passing through the balloon, hung down the side, and the neck of the hydrogen globe was lengthened so that it ended well below the brazier and out of range of its flames.

Still, to launch oneself into the air in a vehicle that brought fire so close to highly explosive hydrogen was so dangerous as to be foolhardy. Pilatre de Rozier and his passenger, Pierre Romain, who had built the balloon, remained outwardly confident as they waited for a favorable wind. Privately, Pilatre de Rozier doubted the wisdom of proceeding, but he had been ordered to make the flight and he could not refuse the King. Early on the morning of June 15 the breeze at last blew gently toward England. The balloon went up.

The strange, mushroom-shaped vehicle climbed rapidly and moved out over the Channel. A witness said later that the gallery appeared slightly out of balance at the outset, but the spectators—Pilatre de Rozier's English fiancée, Susan Dyer, among them—stared entranced as it attained an elevation of some 5,000 feet and appeared to hang motionless. A few moments later a vagrant westerly pushed it back over France. Then—catastrophe.

Flames suddenly leaped from the balloon's crown. Susan Dyer and the other observers, frozen in horror, saw the flame-shrouded balloon plummet earthward. One of the aeronauts yelled something unintelligible through his speaking trumpet to workmen on the ground, then the wicker gallery crashed to earth some 300 feet from the Channel. Pilatre de Rozier died instantly; his wounds included two broken legs and a "violent contusion" in his chest. Romain, suffering multiple injuries, survived only long enough to whisper "Oh, Jesu" before he too perished. Susan Dyer was so shocked by the sight of her young fiancé falling to his death that she herself collapsed and died soon afterward.

Ironically, the most likely cause of the fire was not the flame in the brazier. Several witnesses reported seeing Pilatre de Rozier pull the valve line soon after the balloon rose. Presumably the gas in the sphere was expanding too fast, possibly because of heat from the montgolfier below, and he was trying to discharge hydrogen. Probably the hydrogen was ignited by a spark of static electricity produced when the valve rope rubbed against the balloon or by the opening of the valve itself.

Only 19 months had passed between Pilatre de Rozier's first flight and his last, months during which an entirely new and dangerous science had been explored with dizzying speed. Considering how little the brave pioneers knew of balloons, of ballast, of air currents and of the effects of temperature and humidity on the performance of their aircraft, it was little short of a miracle that there had been no serious injuries before the deaths of Pilatre de Rozier and Romain.

An artistic outpouring inspired by flight

The excitement that swept France with the beginning of the balloon era inspired artisans everywhere, and the record of that heady moment in history is flamboyantly expressed in their surviving work. By December 1783—in time for the traditional season of gift giving—articles of every sort were being created to meet the public demand.

Almost anything, it seemed, could be made in the shape of a balloon or with a balloon motif. The items usually reflected the fanciful ornamentation of the late-rococo period in which they were produced and ranged from intricately designed chests and chairs to such extravagances as perfume bottles and finely beaded slippers.

In the Nevers region of France, noted for its flourishing porcelain industry, craftsmen produced enormous quantities of balloon-decorated plates and bowls. The skilled artists of Strasbourg and Moustiers embellished porcelain cups, saucers and jardinieres with ballooning scenes.

Perhaps the most exquisite manifestations of the ballooning craze, which lasted in less intense form well into the 19th Century, were petite tableaus that were applied to small accessories or were used as decoration on furniture. The scenes were painstakingly assembled from tiny colored glass beads, sometimes as many as a thousand of them to the square inch.

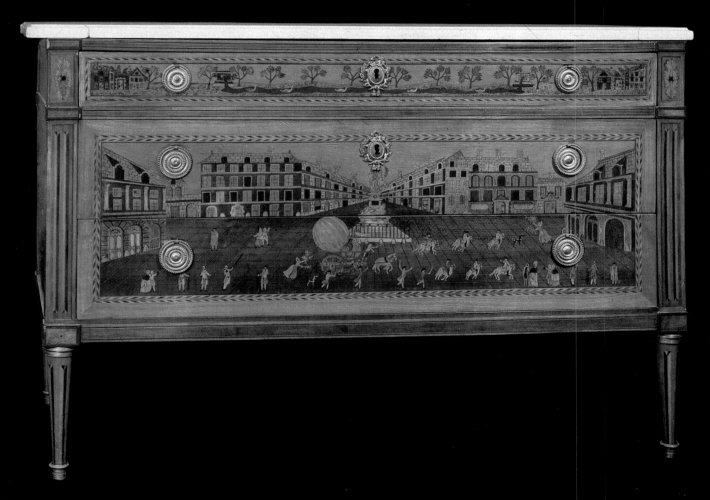

The return of Professor Jacques Charles's balloon to Paris by horse-drawn wagon after his flight in 1783 is shown in the skillfully applied wood-veneer marquetry on this French sideboard.

Like a gracefully hovering jewel, the globe of this chandelier is composed of small crystal sections while the candelabrum, hanging like a gondola below it, is a golden metal adorned with crystal ornaments.

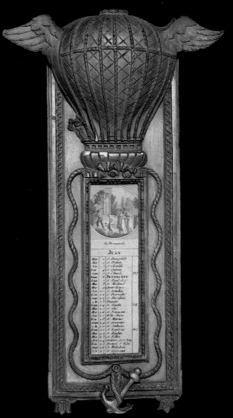

A winged balloon trailing a grapnel decorates this gilded 18th Century French calendar stand of carved wood.

Ballooning scenes enliven the back and the needlepoint seat cover of a finely carved walnut chair from 18th Century France.

The landing of Professor Charles and Noël Robert outside of Paris in December 1783 is depicted in this 1790 clock.

Crafted of two types of gold, this oval box is a showcase for a bone-inlay painting of a montgolfier ascending in the presence of the King and Queen of France.

The balloon-like globe of this elaborate dressing-table ornament from the 19th Century can be opened up to reveal its cache of four small scent bottles.

Romance and ballooning are paired on this painted silk fan from England

The glass beads adorning this small writing desk show Charles greeting the Duke of Chartres after landing. The inscription reads, "My Lord, I am at your service."

The wind, personified by two puffing faces, propels a balloon on the glass-beaded back of this hand screen.

in which courting lovers are flanked by balloon scenes of the 1780s.

A woman's slippers feature a glass-bead representation of the first military observation balloon, L'Entreprenant, used by the French against the Austrians in 1794.

A flight by Vincent Lunardi takes on a three-dimensional quality in this Russian double-walled glass beaker.

Noël Robert and a companion are shown aloft in an early hydrogen balloon on this glazed earthenware plate from Brittany.

A china tureen from early-19th Century England is decorated with a scene that is believed to be a flight of the pioneer British balloonist James Sadler.

An 1803 ascent by Étienne Robertson and the 1819 death fall

Jacques Charles and Noël Robert are painted in glaze on a wine jug with the Latin inscription: "Thus is immortality gained."

The rim of this shaving dish, decorated with the ascent of Charles and Robert, is indented to fit the shaver's neck.

MORT DE MADAME BLANCHARD
1782

of Madame Blanchard, wrongly dated, decorate French tiles.

Charles and Robert fly once again in the carefully rendered gold design on this late-18th Century coffeepot made of white Paris porcelain.

2

Heyday of the high-flying showmen

he balloon is not the master of the atmosphere," wrote a 19th Century historian. "On the contrary, it is its powerless slave." By accepting that slavery—and by frankly exploiting the dangers it implied as part of the spectacle of ballooning—an audacious, foot-loose and hardy collection of early aeronauts learned to make a sustained, if risky, living at their chosen careers. They were professional showmen and, with aristocratic pioneers like Pilatre de Rozier dead and the Montgolfiers and Professor Charles involved in earthbound pursuits, the sky belonged to them.

Two of these itinerant performers appeared almost at once. They were Jean Pierre Blanchard, who had established his reputation in 1785 by ballooning across the English Channel, and Vincent Lunardi, his daring Italian-born contemporary. By the end of the century this pair had introduced the wonders of lighter-than-air flight to the capitals of Europe and even to America. They were the harbingers of a long and colorful line of aeronaut-adventurers who sought their fortunes in the sky.

The balloon itself seemed the perfect symbol of the 19th Century, an unhurried age when technology had not yet telescoped time and distance, when the business and pleasures of life were conducted at a statelier pace. If in later years balloons would continue to be useful, within their limits, and a source of pleasure for thousands, in the 19th Century they were celebrated by the sore-necked multitudes for what they were in the truest sense: the embodiment at once of leisurely grace and of man's dogged aspiration to rise above his element. In Europe, ballooning was the stuff of royal occasions, the coronations of kings, queens and emperors; in the United States, especially during the latter half of the century, a fair or exhibition without a balloon ascent was an event scarcely worth attending, and the shows were just infrequent enough to keep the public's appetite sharp.

In the early years the unadorned spectacle of a balloon going up was thrill enough for the crowds. There was always, of course, the gingery possibility of an accident—nothing too serious, perhaps just a sudden plunge or a moment of danger on the descent. When simply going up and coming back was no longer sufficiently exciting, balloonists began a restless quest for novelty. Ascents on horseback were among the first of the refinements, along with flights at night, often enlivened by displays of fireworks. A female balloonist invariably drew a crowd, especially if her costume was formfitting. Parachute drops, first by caged animals

Symbolic of the 18th Century's glorified view of ballooning as a passage to the heavens, the painting above depicts an encounter in the clouds between the celebrated aeronaut Vincent Lunardi and the mythical gods Zeus and Hera.

and later by human aeronauts, added zest to the show, as did the performances of airborne trapeze artists who dangled precipitously from slender bars 1,000 feet up.

Ballooning was perilous even in the best of circumstances, but these daredevils seemed to court danger—with predictable results. "Had I a thousand lives I would sooner lose them all than be branded with the names of coward and deceiver," declared Vincent Lunardi, the prototype professional whose ascents for the sake of honor often ended in a jarring, wind-driven collision with a hedge or a tree or, on one occasion, a house.

Lunardi and Blanchard, who shared a misguided faith in oars as a steering device, did little to advance the art of aerostation, but others in the professional fraternity did much. The parachute, invented by balloonist André Jacques Garnerin in 1797 and at first considered merely the means for a daring stunt, may well have been ballooning's most

In a carnival atmosphere, Vincent Lunardi's second balloon, painted to resemble the Union Jack, rises in June 1785 from a site at St. George's Fields built expressly for balloon launchings. The huge crowd was described as "the most brilliant assemblage of fashionable people ever collected on a similar occasion."

significant contribution to man's conquest of the air. Introduction of the rip panel permitted immediate deflation of the balloon as a safety measure on landing. And the ingenious drag, or guide, rope, by dragging more or less of its length—and weight—on the ground helped to regulate the balloon's altitude.

Finally, the discovery of a fairly constant, high-altitude current of air flowing from west to east opened the sky to long-distance voyages and to the possibility of drifting across the Atlantic, a thought that fueled the dreams of aeronauts for much of the century. But even the most serious engineers of aeronautic progress, such giants of their day as Charles Green of England and John Wise of the United States, spent most of their time as paid entertainers. For in the end the advancement of ballooning, the forays into science and warfare, and even the great distance flights all were contrapuntal to the main theme of the era. That theme was show business—providing delight for a pleasure-craving public.

"Behold me," exclaimed Vincent Lunardi on September 14, 1784, "exhausted with fatigue, anxiety and distress on the eve of an undertaking that requires my being collected, cool and easy in mind." The 25-year-old Lunardi, who worked at the Italian embassy in London, was not one to underdramatize himself, but there was truth behind his concern. Months earlier he had announced that he intended to make England's first manned balloon flight, only to meet with one setback after another. Once, his balloon had even been impounded, after an argument over money, by the owner of the Lyceum, where it had been on display (Lunardi had to round up a posse of policemen to reclaim it). With lift-off only hours away, it became apparent that his red-and-white hydrogen balloon would not be inflated in time—and 150,000 spectators at the Artillery Ground were waiting with mounting impatience.

At last, a tense hour behind schedule and with his audience on the verge of riot, Lunardi stepped into the rectangular wicker basket and gave the signal "hands off." The Prince of Wales, one of the watchers, removed his hat and stood at solemn attention. The balloon rose into the air and the mob at the gates roared its satisfaction. Considerably more concerned than the crowd about the aeronaut's prospects was King George III. As the balloon floated past his palace window, His Majesty halted a meeting with his ministers to note: "We may resume our deliberations on the subject before us at pleasure, but we may never see poor Lunardi again." At that moment, however, Lunardi was enjoying himself hugely, emptying a bottle of wine "to the health of my friends and benefactors in the lower world."

Lunardi had equipped his balloon with two oars—one of which had been broken in the ascent—and two wings, in the mistaken belief that he could thereby control his horizontal and vertical movement. According to his own account, when he decided it was time to descend Lunardi "rowed" himself, with the remaining oar, down to a field 24 miles from his departure point. Field hands ran in terror at the sight of this "Devil's horse" descending, but a brave young woman—Lunardi had an uncanny knack for attracting them—came readily to his aid. Within hours he was the toast of London.

Lunardi followed up his triumphant maiden voyage with a series of ascents from Liverpool, Glasgow, Edinburgh and other cities in the summer and fall of 1785. His skill at self-promotion was combined with a disarming, self-deprecating charm that endeared the handsome aeronaut to the audience he coveted most: "Praise never gratifies me highly unless I receive it from the fair sex," he confessed, and he was rarely without gratification. His fans donned Lunardi bonnets and Lunardi garters in honor of ballooning's first matinee idol.

But the British public's infatuation with the young Italian soured after a freak accident in the summer of 1786 in which a young man was killed when his arm was caught in the anchor rope of the rising balloon. Perhaps unfairly, Lunardi's once-doting public branded him a greedy and unscrupulous charlatan; he was driven from Britain in disgrace. Though he never returned to the scene of his initial success, Lunardi continued his high-spirited and candid pursuit of fame and glory for some 20 years in other lands. Once, in Spain, he was borne in triumph through the streets of a village whose people had mistaken him for a saint descended from heaven. He was touring Portugal in 1806 when his health deserted him; at the age of 47, he died in a Lisbon convent— first and last at the tender mercies of the fair sex.

"M. Blanchard's 45th aerial flight," promised the advertisement in a 1793 Philadelphia newspaper, "is positively fixed for Wednesday, January 9 in the prison court at 10 in the morning precisely, weather permitting. Send subscription cards to Oeller's Hotel. Price—$5."

Five dollars was a lot of money in post-Revolutionary America, but Jean Pierre Blanchard, the French showman who had made the first airborne crossing of the English Channel eight years earlier, was a name to be reckoned with. Like Vincent Lunardi, Blanchard had become a traveling balloonist *extraordinaire.* He had been the first to venture aloft over Germany, Holland and Belgium (all in 1785), Switzerland (1788) and Poland and Austria (both in 1790). When the French Revolution erupted, Blanchard was jailed in Austria on charges of dispensing seditious propaganda. He managed to escape to the relative calm of the United States, arriving in Philadelphia—then the nation's capital—in December of 1792. Soon he was drumming up trade for the first manned free balloon flight in the New World.

Estimating that the yard of Philadelphia's Walnut Street Prison could hold several thousand spectators, Blanchard hoped to sell 500 tickets at five dollars apiece and at least 1,000 more at two dollars each to cover the costs of his experiment, as he called his ascent. It seemed a reasonable goal: Philadelphia was agog at the prospect of the flight, and the fever had spread to the surrounding countryside as well. On January 8, a pragmatic resident of nearby Woodbury, New Jersey, noted in his

Like many early aeronauts, Vincent Lunardi
became the target of satirists. In this
1784 English print, his balloon is drawn
to resemble a fool's head and his
adventures are ridiculed in verse borrowed
from the poet Alexander Pope.

diary that he had postponed a visit to Philadelphia the next morning because of the balloon mania that gripped the city. "Almost all of Woodbury was going to see it," Samuel Mickle wrote, "which appeared likely to obstruct my business there."

The promised day dawned fair and unseasonably warm. At 9 a.m. the process of inflating the hydrogen balloon began, accompanied by band music and the occasional blast of a cannon. Blanchard could count among his audience not only President George Washington but four of his eventual successors: John Adams, Thomas Jefferson, James Madison and James Monroe. Washington presented Blanchard, who spoke no English, a "passport" with which to identify himself on landing. Shortly after 10 a.m., dapper in a bright blue suit and feathered hat, the aeronaut stepped into his gondola—painted a matching blue and trimmed with spangles—accompanied by a small black dog, and at 10:10 a.m. the two ascended from the prison yard. "I could not help being surprised and astonished," Blanchard wrote afterward, "when I turned my eyes toward the immense number of people who covered the open places, the roofs of the houses, the steeples, the streets and the roads. What a sight! How delicious for me to enjoy it!"

Forty-six minutes and 15 miles later, the aeronaut and his airsick pet dropped down gently near Deptford Township, New Jersey. He presented his passport to a farmer—who could not read. Then Blanchard opened a bottle of wine—a gesture the farmer did understand.

"Great ado," wrote Samuel Mickle in his diary that day, "with looking for and at the balloon which came within one mile from and eastward of us at Woodbury. This is an instance of the body as well as the mind being in ye air. Balloon is ye subject in almost every quarter." Returning to the capital that evening, Blanchard gave President Washington the unique flag he had carried on America's first air voyage—the French tricolor on one side, Stars and Stripes on the other.

During his quarter-century ballooning career, the nomadic Blanchard made 61 ascents in nine countries—but he never felt himself adequately rewarded for his efforts. In Philadelphia, where spectators had thronged the free rooftop perches, gate receipts for the historic ascent had totaled a meager $405. Blanchard's return to Europe in 1798 brought little improvement. In 1800, angered by a tightfisted crowd in Nantes, France, Blanchard threatened to give up aeronautics for good. "I therefore make an end here of my ascents," he declared, "and my aerial flotilla is for sale." Noting that the collection contained "1,800 ells of taffeta of good quality," he advised potential buyers that "these dismembered balloons will make excellent cloaks, caps, aprons and umbrellas." The chastisement must have had some effect, for Blanchard kept his balloons and his career going for another eight years. Then, in 1808, he suffered a heart attack in mid-air. Unconscious, he landed with a thud and, though uninjured, fell into a physical and mental decline that ended with his death in Paris on March 7, 1809.

Blanchard did not live to see his beloved profession enter its most glorious, and profitable, hour, but his wife certainly did—a development that would have astonished the oft destitute showman. "My poor dear," he once said to her, "when I am dead I fear you will have no other resource than to throw yourself into the water." Instead, Madeleine Sophie Armant Blanchard became the first woman successfully to make ballooning her career, continuing to perform for a decade after her husband's death. Extremely petite, she had first soloed in 1805 in a gondola so light and fragile it was described as a child's cradle. Fearless in the air, Madame Blanchard paradoxically was timid on the ground. She refused to ride in carriages, for example, because she was sure they would overturn. Preferring the calmer winds that attended evening ascents, the tiny woman would sometimes stay aloft all night, sleeping in her cradle and descending at dawn—when she could see what awaited her below. Even-handed in her politics, she made an ascension in honor of Napoleon's marriage in 1810 and another, four years later, to celebrate the return to Paris of the Bourbon monarch Louis XVIII.

Damsels who dared the perilous sky

On the ground, 18th and 19th Century women had very few avenues in which they could compete on equal terms with men. But in the air the ladies often matched their male colleagues in daring—and surpassed them in popularity.

The earliest women to go aloft did so for the thrill of it. On June 4, 1784, Elisabeth Thible of France became the first female aeronaut when she cajoled a friend into taking her along on a flight from Lyons. Other women followed her example, and in 1798, Jeanne Labrosse (*below*), later the wife of French balloonist André Jacques Garnerin, became the first woman to pilot a balloon herself.

The discovery that female aeronauts were a novelty that could be turned to profit gave rise in the 1800s to a number of professional women balloonists.

Often they began ballooning in tandem with their husbands, then set out successfully on their own. After her celebrated husband died, plucky Madeleine Sophie Blanchard dazzled Europe with her exploits for a decade until her career was ended by a fatal accident (*overleaf*). Margaret Graham, her roof-skimming misadventures thrilling a generation of English audiences, performed by herself for 15 years after her husband went into semiretirement.

The Garnerins' niece, Elisa, added a dash of peril to some of her ascents by parachuting back to earth. She developed a skill for pinpoint landings, and when one (male) skeptic wagered that she could not land on a specific spot on a windy day, Elisa stunned him by hitting the bull's-eye—and collected the bet.

Jeanne Labrosse Garnerin, the first woman to go up without a male pilot, is the focus of a fashionable audience in this 1802 etching.

Her balloon destroyed by a mid-air fire, Madeleine Blanchard is hurled to her death on a Paris street in 1819. She was the first woman killed in a ballooning mishap.

Invoking the Queen's name, a poster announces an evening ascent by Margaret Graham from the Royal Gardens, a London amusement park, in 1850.

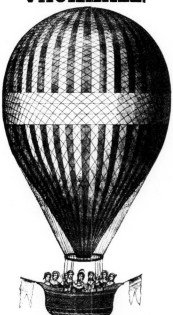

Under the Patronage of Her most Gracious Majesty
THE QUEEN.

ROYAL GARDENS
VAUXHALL.

MRS. GRAHAM
THE ONLY
Female Aeronaut,
ACCOMPANIED BY A
PARTY OF YOUNG LADIES,
WITH THE NEW
BALLOON,
THE ROYAL
"VICTORIA & ALBERT,"
WILL MAKE AN ASCENT FROM THE
ROYAL GARDENS,
VAUXHALL,
ON
THURSDAY next, July 11th, 1850.
NO EXTRA CHARGE.
Doors open at Six o'Clock.   Ascent at Seven.
W. ROCK, Machine Printer, next the Elephant and Castle, Newington.

In a dramatic rescue, the French husband-and-wife team of Jules and Caroline Duruof is saved from the North Sea in 1874 after crashing during a storm.

German aeronauts Gottfried and Wilhelmine Reichardt appear in formal dress in this 1830 portrait. Frau Reichardt's solo ascents were a major attraction at the Prater park in Vienna.

By the time Madame Blanchard took up ballooning, the rivalry between hydrogen and hot-air balloons had resulted in a hands-down victory for hydrogen. Its greater lifting force, combined with improvements in the method of generating the gas, had enabled the hydrogen balloon to overcome its principal liabilities: higher cost and the longer time required for inflation. Madame Blanchard's birdlike size reduced these liabilities even further: Her dainty aerostat filled quickly, at a relatively low cost. Soon her public ascents were turning a nice profit.

But even balloonists who used hydrogen were risk takers by definition, as Madeleine Sophie Blanchard eventually learned. During her evening ascents she often illuminated her performance with a brilliant display of airborne fireworks. On July 7, 1819, while ascending from Tivoli Gardens in Paris, she inadvertently ignited the gas escaping from the balloon's neck. Desperately she fought the flames, and the crowd below burst into applause at what looked like a spectacular part of the act—only to watch in horror as the balloon crashed on a roof where her frail wicker car overturned, sending her plummeting to her death.

Two years later, an English aeronaut introduced a new lifting element to ballooning. Charles Green filled his balloon with coal gas, a mixture of hydrogen and methane that resulted from the heat processing of bituminous coal. Increasingly available from the public gas mains that were being installed to provide lighting for cities, coal gas cost far less than pure hydrogen; it could fill a balloon in two or three hours instead of a day or more and, being denser, was far slower to permeate a balloon's cloth envelope and escape. Though hydrogen continued in use, common coal gas would be the fuel to carry most of the next generation of aeronauts on their gloriously impractical adventures.

Charles Green was England's premier balloonist during the first half of the 19th Century. The son of a London fruit merchant, he was 36 years old in 1821 when he went aloft for the first time. A jovial and gracious man on the ground, Green turned into a no-nonsense taskmaster in the air, a metamorphosis that dumfounded his passengers. "He was taciturn and almost irritable," one passenger wrote of Green's airborne demeanor, but after the flight "he was garrulous, and delighting all with his intelligence, his enterprise, his enthusiasm, and his courtesy."

Green embraced the air as his natural element and piloted his balloons with consummate skill. Indeed, over a 31-year career he was said to have reduced the risky art to a veritable routine. Whenever possible, he connected a hose from the nearest gas main to his balloon and in a short time his craft would be ready to go. A fastidious technician by temperament, he became a performer by economic necessity. He hopscotched the English countryside, announcing his ascents in advance and showing up promptly to greet the public in his good-natured style. The broadsides of his day convey the flavor: "Fete! Fun! Balloon Inflation! Ascent! Fireworks! Etc. Only ONE SHILLING." For those who attended on Sunday there was no admission charge—"but every

Planning the epic venture that took them across Western Europe in the Royal Vauxhall in 1836, balloonist Charles Green (far right) confers with his partners Thomas Monck Mason (standing, right) and Robert Hollond (seated, center), in the company of three other friends.

visitor is expected to take refreshment to the amount of sixpence.''

Green used all kinds of innovations to keep his performances lively. One of his earliest triumphs was an ascent on a pony attached by ropes to the balloon's hoop; he calmed the animal by feeding it beans from his hand. A planned flight in the company of a tiger and its trainer was canceled when the authorities intervened. Lucky lottery winners were treated to a ride with the master balloonist, and he went up on one occasion with a detachment of military musicians. Another time he was joined by a music-hall singer who regaled the fans below with such popular songs of the day as ''Hot Codlins'' and ''Pigs' Pettitoes.''

By 1835 the 50-year-old Green had logged some 6,000 miles on 200 ascents. He had seen more of his native isle, from better vantages, than any man before him. And, after 240 hours in the air, he had learned what he wanted in a balloon. With the financial backing of the proprietors of London's Vauxhall Gardens, he set about designing the perfect aerostat. The result, named for its owners the *Royal Vauxhall,* was a red-and-white marvel of imported Italian silk that stood 80 feet high from its

eagle-prowed car to its crown. Its long tapering gores of silk were sealed with a special adhesive Green had invented to strengthen the seams.

On its maiden flight in 1836, the *Royal Vauxhall* lifted nine passengers to an elevation of 13,000 feet in just five minutes. The balloon was magnificent. All it lacked was a challenge worthy of it—and that was soon supplied by two of Green's most avid fans. A member of Parliament named Robert Hollond—who would bankroll the project—and Thomas Monck Mason, an Irish theatrical producer, persuaded Green to aim the *Royal Vauxhall* at the Continent, with them on board, and see how far they might go. The result was ballooning's most dramatic achievement to that point.

Green prepared for the adventure with even more than his customary care. His most important innovation for the flight was a drop rope 1,000 feet long, an idea that had been suggested earlier but never tried. Green believed that the rope, controlled by a winch in the car, would conserve ballast and lessen the danger of crashing into high ground when flying at night. When the rope—which was also equipped with copper floats— dragged on the ground or in the water, it would relieve the balloon of the

In a mid-19th Century engraving that pokes friendly fun at Charles Green's penchant for ballooning ever farther from England, Green (in light coat, center) is shown introducing his party of aeronauts to people of the Antipodes Islands, in the South Pacific—at the opposite end of the earth.

part of its weight that dragged. As the balloon then ascended, the rope would have the reverse effect, adding weight and checking the climb.

Hollond, Mason and Green ascended from Vauxhall early on the afternoon of November 7, 1836, caught a northwest breeze and sailed serenely over the Kent countryside, then past Dover and out over the Channel. "Behind us," wrote Mason, "the whole line of English coast, its white cliffs melting into obscurity, appeared sparkling with scattered lights." Through the deepening dusk, they watched solitary ships cross the dark water below. In another hour they were abreast of Calais at 3,000 feet, dining sumptuously on cold beef, ham, fowl and tongue, "together with a due admixture of wine and other liquors." Soon, like bonfires on a distant plain, the blast furnaces of the ironworks at Liége, Belgium, passed beneath them. Then came a darkness so absolute that it was nearly palpable. Mason had the impression they were "cleaving our way through an interminable mass of black marble which, solid a few inches before us, seemed to soften as we approached."

The welcome sunrise yielded a vista of snow fields. They had crossed a slice of France and most of Belgium and now were over the duchy of Nassau, in present-day West Germany. Alternately valving and throwing out ballast as he maneuvered amid low-altitude winds, Green finally brought the *Royal Vauxhall* to rest near the town of Weilburg. It was 7:30 a.m.—18 hours since their departure—and they had come 380 miles from London, the longest flight to that time. Local acclaim for their feat was immediate and overwhelming. "Balls, dinners, concerts and other amusements were given without intermission," wrote Mason. Charles Green was crowned with a laurel wreath and his balloon, at a ceremony attended by the noble families of the duchy, was rechristened *The Great Balloon of Nassau.*

The voyage to Nassau fired Green's imagination with the possibility of a flight across the Atlantic itself. Noting that he had found a constant west-to-east air current at an elevation of roughly 10,000 feet, Green suggested that "wealthy patrons of the art" underwrite his attempt to launch the *Nassau* from North America and ride this current to England. In 1839 and again in 1846 he floated this idea, but despite his solid reputation the appeal failed to spark a rush of investors. So Green returned each time to the business of giving aerial tours to paying customers. By 1852, when at age 67 he embarked on a series of sentimental "final" ascents, he had made more than 500 flights. He retained his stern airborne demeanor to the end. After negotiating a difficult landing on his final "final" flight, "the old ethereal pilot," as an admirer called him, saw that his passengers were starting to climb out before the balloon had settled. "Sit down, all of you," he barked. And they obeyed.

During his long reign as undisputed champion of the skies, Charles Green did have some rather eccentric competition from the singular husband-and-wife team of George and Margaret Graham. The Grahams, it may be said, specialized in fiascoes. But the crowds loved them,

A gas balloon's simple components

This drawing identifies the basic components of a gas balloon. Its envelope, usually made of a tightly woven fabric, is coated with varnish or a rubber solution in order to increase its resistance to rips and to retard the escape of gas. A netting of hemp covering the envelope uniformly distributes the weight of the basket, which hangs from a suspension hoop.

The balloon is inflated through an opening at its bottom and, once released, ascends until its weight is in equilibrium with the air around it. Sandbag ballast is dropped to make the balloon rise higher, and gas is released by valve to cause it to descend. Near the ground, the trailing drag rope helps, by its weight, to control altitude.

Once committed to landing, the balloonist can pull the rip panel, collapsing the envelope rapidly so the balloon will not drag along the ground—or accidentally lift off again.

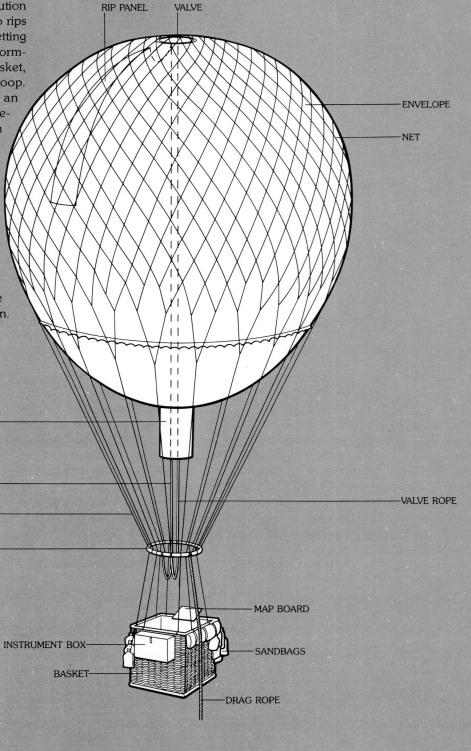

RIP PANEL VALVE

ENVELOPE

NET

INFLATING APPENDIX

RIP-PANEL ROPE

SUSPENSION ROPE

SUSPENSION HOOP

VALVE ROPE

MAP BOARD

INSTRUMENT BOX

SANDBAGS

BASKET

DRAG ROPE

for they seldom failed to produce a sensation—and a broken bone or two. One of their disaster-shortened flights left a row of houses remodeled by the balloon's trailing grapnel (a small anchor with several flukes) and left the Grahams themselves lying dazed on a roof. Another flight, during coronation festivities for Queen Victoria in 1838, had more serious consequences: This time the grapnel collided with a house, dislodging a large stone that fell upon and killed an unwary passerby. After this tragedy, George Graham, who was much older than his wife, rarely took to the air, taking over the business side of the partnership instead.

Margaret Graham, "rather a heavy person," by one account, "weighing about 200 pounds," was as adept at self-promotion as she seemed to be ill-starred at aerostation. Her written versions of her exploits were often at odds with the reports of unbiased witnesses—especially where accidents were concerned—but they made good newspaper copy and kept the crowds coming. She would usually begin her performances in enclosed courtyards or tea gardens—where she could more easily collect fees from those who wished a close-up view of the balloon. Once airborne, she would descend only after she was out of sight, whereupon George Graham would pick her up in a carriage and transport her back to her waiting public. This dramatic reappearance of Her Majesty's Only Female Aeronaut, as she styled herself, never failed to draw tremendous applause.

Perhaps the closest of Margaret Graham's brushes with death came not in the air but on the ground. After the balloon had landed safely on an 1850 flight, its discharging gas caught fire and she suffered severe burns on her face and hands. When she recovered, she gamely continued in her chosen career—which in all lasted some 30 remarkable years—often taking one or more of her seven children along for the ride. And in the end she died peacefully in her bed.

The United States's first home-grown professional balloonist had a much briefer—if less accident prone—career. On September 9, 1830, Charles Ferson Durant made the first of the 12 ascents he would accomplish over the next four years, lifting off in late afternoon from New York City's Castle Garden (now Battery Park). As he rose above the 30,000 upturned faces in the crowd, he let fall in his wake printed copies of "The Aeronaut's Address," six verses of doggerel, redolent with aerial bravado, that he had composed. One stanza will suffice:

> Perhaps I may touch at the moon
> To give your respects as I pass, sirs,
> And learn if the spheres are in tune
> Or if they are lighted with gas, sirs.

As he drifted over Staten Island, Durant dropped a note to some friends, promising them that he would be by for tea a little later. The flight ended safely in South Amboy, New Jersey—having covered 30 miles in one hour and 20 minutes. Durant dispatched carrier pigeons to carry word of his triumph back to New York.

The 25-year-old Durant, who had grown up in nearby Jersey City, was a gregarious troubadour of the air and a man of parts. In later years he would pursue varied careers as a printer-lithographer, a silkworm culturalist (he produced the first silk known to be made in the United States) and an amateur marine biologist. His "colloquial powers and social qualities," a contemporary wrote, made him "a truly companionable man." Durant had learned ballooning in France, and he proved an apt pupil; on one flight, from Baltimore, he succeeded in landing adroitly on the deck of a steamer in Chesapeake Bay. The only blemish on his record, in fact, was an unscheduled 1834 splashdown in Boston Harbor—where he floated placidly in his "gum-elastic" life preserver until he was rescued. Durant was only 29 when he retired from the air, but his skill and enthusiasm had inspired a passion for ballooning in America that would persist through the 19th Century—and that found its first

Premier American aeronaut John Wise had unshakable faith in balloons as the superior form of transport. In 1847 he wrote: "Our children will travel to any part of the globe without the inconvenience of smoke, sparks and seasickness, and at the rate of 100 miles per hour."

great protagonist in a Pennsylvania cabinetmaker named John Wise. Wise was born in Lancaster, Pennsylvania, in February 1808, the month and year in which Jean Pierre Blanchard made his last ascent. At 14 he read an account of a balloon voyage in Italy and began building model hot-air fire balloons—once setting a neighbor's house ablaze. The boyhood infatuation grew into a lifelong love affair with flight. "This was more than grandeur," he wrote after his initial ascent, in 1835, when he was 27. "All the higher faculties of the mind become gradually aroused; I was gently awakening from a magnificent dream."

Long-faced and somewhat Lincolnesque in appearance, Wise was in equal parts romantic and mechanic—the ideal blend for an aeronaut. The journal he kept during all his flights was by turns a paean to aerostation and a laconic description of his scientific experiments. On one Fourth of July ascent from Lebanon, Pennsylvania, his valve line became entangled in the rigging and broke off at a point beyond his reach. Unable to release gas, he rode upward, out of control, until the outward pressure burst a hole in the bottom of the balloon. Then down it fell in what Wise coolly described as a "tolerably rapid descent."

Throwing out his remaining ballast, he managed a safe landing, though admitting later that for a few tense minutes he feared "it might be my last voyage." Wise decided to learn from the experience; some time later he repeated the incident, deliberately causing his balloon to burst in mid-flight. He was intrigued, and relieved, to see that the torn balloon, emptied of its gas, formed a parachute-like canopy against the top of its encircling net, enabling him to land with only a modest bump.

As a result of such experiments, Wise developed the rip panel, a section of the balloon envelope that could be opened instantly by yanking a special cord; this permitted fast deflation on landing and eliminated the risk of hedgehopping by partially deflated balloons caught in ground-level gusts. Wise also put the rip panel to a more spectacular use. Yanking the rip cord while still well above the ground, he thrilled his audiences by, in effect, parachuting steeply to earth.

Unlike many of his European counterparts, Wise enjoyed remarkably trouble-free relations with the crowds that came to see him. On the few occasions when he failed to ascend because of weather or problems with the balloon, he wrote, "no evil consequences except my extreme mortification ensued from the disappointment." Once, when he offered to take riders aloft in his tethered balloon, the crowd's initial reluctance, he reported, turned to "a perfect mania." In an effort to stem the tide, he began charging a fee. At 25 cents a trip the customers continued to press in, as they did when he upped the ante to 50 cents. The aeronaut collected $80 before the crush made further operations impossible.

Though Wise was soon in great demand at the nation's summer playgrounds, his dream was to ride a westerly wind across the Atlantic. Like Charles Green, he had discovered by 1842 "that a current from West to East in the atmosphere is constantly in motion within the height of 12,000 feet above the ocean. Nearly all my trips are strong proof of

Advertising takes to the air

The use of balloons to sell products and services was a 19th Century innovation that blossomed, fittingly, in Frankfurt, Germany, historically a center for trade fairs and exhibitions; it soon spread to other German cities as well.

Beginning in the 1880s, the managers of the Frankfurt Zoo exploited the balloon's proven power to attract a crowd by regularly scheduling ascents from the zoo grounds. The result was a handsome increase in paid attendance. The natural next step was to paint advertisements on the balloons, in letters large enough to be read from the ground.

The most enterprising aerial advertiser was Georg Rodeck, a self-commissioned "captain" of ballooning who throughout the late 1880s and 1890s rented his balloon to any firm that wanted its message proclaimed from the sky. Rodeck supplemented his income on each tethered flight by taking up paying passengers in the advertisement-decorated balloon.

Rodeck's commercial success was not lost on Germany's most prominent balloonist of the day, Käthchen Paulus. Billed as the "Heavenly Phenomenon," Fraulein Paulus was famous for her free flights and breathtaking parachute descents. But the admission fees too often failed to match her expenses, so she turned her balloon into an airborne billboard in order to make ends meet.

An advertisement for meat extract and peptone adorns "Captain" Georg Rodeck's balloon Hammonia in this 1889 poster printed to publicize Hamburg's Exhibition of Applied Arts and Industry.

The Hamburg-America Line rented Rodeck's balloon at the International Electrotechnical Display in 1891 to advertise its swift 7½-day passage to New York.

Käthchen Paulus advertises herself and Adler bicycles in this 1899 poster for an ascent from the Frankfurt Zoo. The device she is shown pedaling had no effect on the balloon's performance.

this.'' Unlike Green, Wise did acquire a financial angel, a Vermont businessman named O. A. Gager, to underwrite his dream. By this time it was 1859, and John Wise was 51 years old. Before daring the ocean, he decided to test fly his new balloon, the *Atlantic,* from St. Louis to the East Coast—a flight that, if successful, would more than double Green's record 380-mile journey in the *Royal Vauxhall.* As it turned out, the *Atlantic's* voyage was one of the great balloon adventures of all time.

The *Atlantic* was large—120 feet high and 60 in diameter—and was equipped with a wooden lifeboat beneath the basket in addition to bountiful supplies of food, wine, lemonade and 1,000 pounds of sand ballast; it also carried a sack of express mail. Wise rode in the wicker car while his three crewmen—Gager, 29-year-old John LaMountain, who had built the balloon, and St. Louis journalist William Hyde—made themselves as comfortable as they could in the boat. The journey began at dusk on July 1, 1859, from St. Louis' Washington Square; for the first few hours it was a dreamlike passage through the star-brushed evening. Illinois slumbered below them and then Indiana. Shortly after dawn they crossed the shore of Lake Erie near Sandusky, Ohio, still heading east; by 11 a.m. they were at the opposite shore—and drifting into trouble. They had spent their ballast lavishly during the night to ride the high-altitude westerly current. Even more alarming was the fact that a wind strong enough to snap tree limbs was raking the ground far below; they would need to stay high to avoid being dashed to pieces. As it was, they were heading out over Lake Ontario at some 90 miles an hour. The moist and cooler air over the lake would inevitably cause them to descend into the storm, and they lacked the ballast to lighten the ship.

LaMountain began to jettison the contents of the boat as they dropped closer to the water, at times skimming just above waves 10 feet high. The *Atlantic* angled repeatedly toward the lake, only to rise again as the crew frantically discarded valises, the mailbag, food and the champagne they were saving for a post-flight celebration. Hyde and Gager hustled into the basket with Wise while LaMountain stripped the boat's lining and threw the planks overboard. Disaster seemed imminent. Wise, fearing that a landing ashore might be even more hazardous, suggested that they swamp the balloon and take their chances in what was left of the boat, but the others overruled him. ''If we are to die let us die on land,'' said Hyde, adding ''if we can reach it.'' Alternately dipping and surging upward in the furious gusts, the balloon skittered just beyond the reach of the whitecaps for what seemed an eternity. LaMountain abandoned the boat and joined the others in peering anxiously at the horizon, straining to glimpse the first sign of land.

At last the shoreline appeared through the spray. It was 1:35 p.m. Wise threw out the heavy iron grapnel as they crossed the beach and entered a dense forest at treetop level, but the flukes of the grapnel simply broke off any tree limbs they snagged upon. The balloon, Wise wrote, ''was like a leviathan tied to a fishhook.'' For a mile it slammed through the forest while the aeronauts rolled around in the car and tried

Félix Tournachon, a Frenchman who was known professionally as Nadar, combined his vocation, photography, with his passion, ballooning, to become the first aerial photographer in the world. He is shown ''raising photography to the height of art'' in this 1862 caricature.

This view of l'Étoile in Paris, taken by Nadar in 1868 from a balloon tethered at 1,700 feet, was the first aerial photograph ever published. Earlier, Nadar had patented his idea for what is now known as air survey: using a series of overlapping aerial photographs to map the land.

to hang on. Gas spewed from dozens of puncture holes in the envelope.

One final squall hurled the balloon against a high tree, where it expired. The basket lodged in a fork about 20 feet up. Cautiously the men inspected themselves. LaMountain had suffered contusions on one hip; the other three were shaken but unhurt. Lowering themselves by ropes, they were greeted by a dumfounded delegation of citizens from the nearby town of Henderson, New York. An elderly lady expressed surprise to see "so sensible-looking a party" debarking from "such an outlandish-looking vehicle." She asked where they had come from. "St. Louis," Wise replied. The lady fixed him with the gimlet gaze of an experienced detector of humbugs. "That will do, now," she said.

The storm-blown *Atlantic* had set a new distance record of 809 miles in 19 hours and 50 minutes—a mark that would stand to the end of the century. Wise had satisfied himself as to the constancy of the west-to-east air current and he immediately hailed his trip as "the greatest balloon voyage that was ever made." Yet the balloon itself was in tatters, and so, for now, was his dream of crossing the ocean. Neither Gager nor anyone else was eager to invest any more capital in his plan.

Over the next two years, other entrants made their bids for glory in the transatlantic derby. In each case they were thwarted without ever seeing the ocean. John LaMountain acquired the wreck of the *Atlantic* and repaired it. But on a test flight from upstate New York he drifted north over Canada and, when forced down, was stranded in the wilderness for four days before he was rescued. Unfortunate timing was the undoing of another candidate, a lanky young New Englander named Thaddeus Lowe. Lowe set out—as John Wise had—to test the west-to-east current on a flight from the Midwest to the Atlantic Coast. He took off from Cincinnati and came down nine hours later near Unionville, South Carolina. The date was April 19, 1861, seven days after the first salvos of the American Civil War had been fired at Fort Sumter. Lowe was seized as a Yankee spy, and was released only after a local innkeeper remembered him as the man who had taken him for a balloon ride a year earlier. Before long, the Carolinians would rue the decision to liberate their prisoner. Thaddeus Lowe would find the glory he craved as commander of the Union Army balloon corps.

The Civil War interrupted American exhibition ballooning for the duration, but in mid-century Europe there was a party going on, and balloons were the guests of honor. "Aerostation has become the legitimate property of the caterers for the amusement of the public," a London newspaper sniffed in 1850. Balloonists were superstars; their autographs were cherished. The crowds gaped in wonder at death-defying acrobats, at ballerinas dangling from cardboard clouds and at the gaudy, glorious balloons themselves. When a female inmate of a London workhouse was asked what she wanted for her 100th birthday, she replied that she fancied a ride in a balloon, and she got one.

European promoters dedicated themselves to the theory that bigger is better, building larger and larger balloons in which to offer rides to the public. *Le Géant (The Giant),* first of a generation of mammoth balloons, was unveiled in Paris in 1863. The aerostat, 196 feet high, was the brain child of pioneer photographer Félix Tournachon, who called himself Nadar; it was concocted as a money-maker to finance experiments in Nadar's other interest—heavier-than-air flying machines.

Le Géant boasted the most elaborate balloon car ever devised. In fact, to call it a car does it a disservice; it was an airborne cottage. Made of wicker, two stories high with a balcony on its roof, it contained six compartments: two cabins, a printing room, a photographic office, a lavatory and a storeroom. The balloon made two ascents from Paris in October of 1863, attracting the largest crowds for any aeronautical event since the historic flight of Jacques Charles 80 years before. But it was just as well that the crowds were not around for the landings.

Nadar and his two deputies, the ballooning brothers Jules and Louis Godard, carried 12 eager passengers on *Le Géant's* much-publicized maiden voyage on October 4. By the time they lifted off, late in the afternoon, the spectators had become so impatient with the tedious inflation process that they watched the ascent in petulant silence. Anticipating an all-night ride across Europe, the passengers had thoughtfully provided themselves with guidebooks and passports, but it was soon evident that they would not need them: The balloon dropped violently to earth after only 15 miles, dragging the wicker bungalow on its side for a bone-rattling mile.

If the first flight was a disappointment, the second, a fortnight later, was a catastrophe. The audience for this ascent, estimated at half a million, included both the Emperor Napoleon III and the King of Greece. Again the lift-off was delayed, but this time the great balloon sailed gracefully off to the northeast, climbing easily to an altitude of 4,000 feet. The six passengers and three crewmen repaired to the balcony for a fine meal as the balloon floated toward Belgium, then over the Netherlands and into Germany. By dawn they had traveled some 400 miles. As they watched a brilliant sunrise, Nadar, fearing that the sun's heat would cause the balloon to burst, ordered a descent.

Suddenly the idyll was transformed into a roller-coaster ride as the monster balloon encountered strong winds near the ground. They had valved gas so liberally on the way down that they were unable to reascend. *Le Géant* bounded across woods and fields, tearing through trees and bouncing off the earth, Nadar said, "like an India rubber ball from the hands of an indefatigable player." Nadar saw to his dismay that they were on a collision course with a railroad train. "A few more revolutions of the wheels and it will all be over," he wrote in a fervid memoir. "A single cry escapes our throats, but what a cry!" The engineer whistled in reply and halted the train with feet to spare. Moments later the runaway balloon finally stopped at the edge of a wood, and burst. The passengers, most of whom had jumped or had been thrown from the car, were strewn over the ground like so many fallen apples.

A throng in Brussels watches Le Géant ascend in September 1864. Some 300 seamstresses had assembled its 22,000 yards of silk.

Several had suffered broken bones, but all—miraculously—survived.

Nadar's unwieldy balloon gave giantism an unsavory reputation that persisted for several years. But by 1867 the French welcomed the introduction of a new balloon, large enough to carry 20 people, that had been designed by a remarkably inventive engineer named Henri Giffard. Like Nadar, Giffard hoped to raise enough money by offering rides—at 20 francs for 10 minutes—to support serious research into powered flight. Attached to a 1,000-foot-long cable, his "first railway station from Paris to the moon" was a popular attraction for two seasons. Even Napoleon III was persuaded to take a ride, though rumor had it that the Emperor spent the entire trip seated regally on the floor.

Giffard's ultimate contribution to giantism was a phenomenally successful creation he called *Le Grand Ballon Captif,* which was exhibited at the 1878 Paris world's fair. Thirty feet higher than the Arc de Triomphe, *Le Captif* was attached to a 2,000-foot-long cable powered by a steam-driven winch. Its comfortable circular car could carry as many as 52 people at a time to an elevation at which they could enjoy an unsurpassed panoramic view of the City of Light. Passengers concerned about vertigo were advised "not to follow the cable while it unwinds" but to focus on either the horizon or the balloon above them. By the end of the fair *Le Captif* had borne aloft 35,000 enchanted passengers—more by far than any other vehicle before it.

The end of the Civil War had brought a revival of civilian ballooning in the United States and with it, inevitably, a revival of the elusive dream of flying the ocean. Show business paid the bills for the now-aging John Wise and his successors, but it was the idea of crossing the Atlantic that kept them interested. An agile balloonist-acrobat named Washington Donaldson, who had once walked a tightrope across Niagara Falls, was particularly eager. In 1873 he and Wise secured the backing of the New York *Daily Illustrated Graphic* for what would be the last major assault on the ocean in the 19th Century. A balloon 160 feet high with an enclosed two-story car was built to the aeronauts' specifications, and passports for a dozen European countries were acquired.

Then everything went wrong. The first disappointment came when the 65-year-old Wise, apparently disgruntled by the *Graphic's* management of the preparations, withdrew from the enterprise. Then the balloon proved too big to be inflated by the facilities available; it was replaced by one only half the original's size, with an open boat for a gondola. When Donaldson finally took off from Brooklyn a few weeks later with two companions, Europe-bound, he traveled barely 100 miles before being forced down in a rainstorm on a farm near North Canaan, Connecticut. The three men had been airborne four hours.

True to the never-say-die code of his aerial brethren, Donaldson declared dramatically that "I will yet do this thing." But he would never get another chance. For the next two years he became the virtual property of P. T. Barnum, the freak-show entrepreneur. Under Barnum's

Adventuresome journalists cram the car of Henri Giffard's enormous hydrogen balloon, Le Captif, at the start of a demonstration flight during the Universal Exhibition in Paris in 1878. The largest balloon built to that time, Le Captif had a capacity of 884,250 cubic feet and took three days to fill.

auspices, Donaldson barnstormed the country, ascending by balloon in flesh-colored tights with one hand languidly gripping a trapeze bar. For added excitement he would pretend to fall and at the last second grab a rope while the spectators gasped. When a reporter asked him why he took such risks he replied with the hard-won cynicism of the profession-al stunt man. "It pays," he said. "People flock in thousands to see me break my neck." His most publicized stunt was an aerial wedding over Cincinnati. Formally attired, Donaldson piloted the balloon while the presiding minister, unable to resist the pun, prayed that the happy couple would always be "lifted above the adversities of life."

Donaldson's ascents became progressively more reckless, as if he were deliberately tampering with the odds on survival. In June of 1875 he was rescued from Lake Ontario after setting out from Toronto in a leaky balloon. A month later, the odds caught up with Barnum's daring young man. On his 139th flight, Donaldson and a reporter named Newton S. Grimwood took off from Chicago and drifted into a storm over Lake Michigan. A month later, the body of the reporter was recovered from a beach. Donaldson's body was never found.

A banner stretched above the bustling traffic of Broadway in 1873 heralds The Daily Graphic, a transatlantic balloon that was named for its sponsor, a New York newspaper. Launched that October, the balloon never made it as far as the sea, landing instead in Connecticut.

Four years later, Lake Michigan claimed another distinguished victim. John Wise, still ballooning at the age of 71, took off for a flight across the lake, and never returned.

At a Fourth of July celebration in 1880 in Little Falls, New York, the last of the famous performing balloonists of the 1800s made her debut. The novice aeronaut was a spirited New Englander named Mary Breed Hawley Myers—known to her public as the "aerial Princess Carlotta." A gold-trimmed flight suit was an integral part of her act, displaying to advantage what one reporter described as "the entire proportions of her youthful figure." When a less captivated reporter had the temerity to describe her as "28 to 30, plain and strong," Carlotta expressed a desire to meet the unchivalrous scribe and "cheer his soul with a weak smile."

Carlotta developed a mastery of her craft akin to genius and for 11 years played the fair circuit without serious injury. She honed her skills by testing the balloons and other aeronautical wonders built by her husband, Carl Myers, at their spacious Balloon Farm near Utica, New York. Their dedication to ballooning was total. When a daughter was born to them in the spring of 1881 she was christened Elizabeth Aerial—and Carlotta was back in the air in time to launch her second ballooning season with a Fourth of July double-header, making two ascents in one day. (Little Elizabeth Aerial lived up to her name, going up with Carlotta for the first time at the age of three, and again at the age of seven; as a young adult she successfully demonstrated a foot-pedaled dirigible, invented by her father, at the St. Louis Exposition of 1903.)

Carlotta's stylish ascents and precision landings were hugely popular. Her exhibitions began setting attendance records everywhere, and she expanded her act to include a trapeze artist. During one double ascension, with Carlotta in the *Skylark* and the aerial gymnast Edwin Clarage in the *Flying Cloud,* the two balloons tarried near each other for half an hour. Then, according to one report, "on various currents they floated about higher and lower, further and nearer like two butterflies," with Clarage performing gymnastics on his trapeze the whole time. The aeronauts discovered that, even when they were three or four miles apart, they could continue to converse easily with each other.

"My balloon was plump full," Carlotta reported in describing the phenomenon, "as was also the *Flying Cloud,* and every sound made by Clarage seemed to come from the mouth of my own balloon, the *Skylark,* just like a telephone. I got so interested in our conversation that I almost neglected to attend to my own balloon properly."

Carlotta retired in 1891, at the age of 42. "She retires from the field," Carl Myers boasted, "with a record of having made more ascensions than all other women combined throughout the world, and more than any man living in America." Like John Wise, her predecessor as America's premier exhibition balloonist, and all the mettlesome performers with whom they shared the skies, Carlotta had found in the air, as Wise had written, "a new life, a new spirit, a new world." ∿

The opening of Japan to American and European influences in the middle of the 19th Century set off a surge of interest there in Western clothes, customs, technology—and balloons. In order to satisfy the public appetite for all of these things, Japanese artists produced woodcut prints like the triptych below. All the prints featured gaily decorated balloons soaring over Western-style buildings in the foreign quarter of Tokyo, called Tsukiji, which was occupied by Westerners dressed in the latest, enviable fashions.

French sporting balloons were the Japanese ideal until France lost the Franco-Prussian War of 1870-1871. After that, Japan followed the German example, studying the Kaiser's balloon technology and eventually creating a military balloon corps based on the Prussian model. As a result, Japan's military balloonists were ready when their country went to war with Russia in 1904.

An American family watches from its bayside terrace as Japanese balloons float over the foreign quarter of Tokyo in this 1877 woodcut.

Dignitaries and seamen cheer as Japan's first military balloon, made of 1,400 yards of paper with a rubber coating, is tested at the Naval Ministry in 1877,

small parachute floating mysteriously in its rigging. Japanese characters explain that the locomotive at right brought gas for the balloon.

3

An unlikely recruit for war

On June 2, 1794, Dutch and Austrian troops who were bombarding the French Revolutionary forces at Maubeuge, near the Belgian border, watched in fear and wonder as a plump balloon rose on mooring lines to an altitude of several hundred feet above the besieged town. Two blue-uniformed Frenchmen were perched in the gently swaying basket that dangled from the craft's rigging, beyond the reach of musketry or cannon fire. There could be no mistake about their mission: While one of them scanned the hostile camp through a telescope, the other made notes on enemy troop dispositions and gun emplacements.

Pulled back to earth by their bustling ground crew, the aerial observers gave their commander an accurate and up-to-the-minute report on the forces ranged against him. For the first time in history, a balloon had been used as an instrument of war.

Balloons are unlikely combatants. The good soldier's virtues of discipline, obedience and dependability are plainly alien to a craft that must yield to every wayward gust and sudden storm. Even so, balloons have performed military missions under a dozen flags since those turbulent years just after the French Revolution. Balloons served both North and South in the American Civil War. They aided the French in the Franco-Prussian conflict of 1870 and 1871 and they bobbed by the hundreds above the trenches of World War I. A generation later, banks of tethered barrage balloons helped to keep low-flying German bombers away from London and other vital targets during World War II. In that war the Japanese dispatched waves of bomb-bearing balloons across the Pacific Ocean in a vain attempt to terrorize the American home front. Later, during the so-called Cold War, balloons were used by the West to loft propaganda leaflets over the Iron Curtain and into Soviet-bloc nations of Eastern Europe.

The potential of balloons as instruments of war had been foreseen by Joseph Montgolfier even before he and his brother Étienne publicly launched their first hot-air balloons in 1783. From the air, Montgolfier predicted, French troops could launch a surprise attack and seize strategically located Gibraltar from the British. "By making the balloons' bag large enough," he calculated grandly, "it will be possible to introduce into Gibraltar an entire army, which, borne by the wind, will enter right above the heads of the English." Montgolfier's bold concept remained no more than that—and the British retained Gibraltar.

Garbed in mourning and standing among symbols of war, a woman representing Paris besieged reaches out by balloon to the world beyond fortified Mont Valérien (background). The painting was done by French symbolist Pierre Puvis de Chavannes during the Prussian siege of 1870, when balloons and their pilots provided a life line between Paris and the outside world.

A more feasible military possibility occurred to another Frenchman, André Giroud de Villette, who had been a passenger on one of the early captive ascents made by François Pilatre de Rozier in Paris. Balloon observers, he wrote, could spot "the positions of an enemy, his movements, his advances and his dispositions," and signal this intelligence back to headquarters. The fertile mind of Benjamin Franklin carried these ruminations a step further: He envisioned an armada of 5,000 balloons, bearing two men each, that would drop from the clouds onto enemy territory—the first airborne division. Franklin doubted that any general could field enough troops to counter such an unpredictable invasion; he even hoped that such a dread prospect might make war unthinkable. The contemporary English writer Horace Walpole also devoted some thought to the balloon's military future. Speculating about prospective uses of the devices he called "mechanic meteors," Walpole hoped that they would not be "converted into new engines of destruction to the human race." But he went on to observe glumly that "the wicked wit of man always studies to apply the results of his talents to enslaving, destroying or cheating his fellow creatures."

Pressed by circumstance, France took an early lead in military ballooning. In the years immediately following the Revolution of 1789 the fragile republican regime was at war almost constantly with the powerful monarchies of Austria, Prussia and Holland. Desperate French officials were willing to hear counsel from any quarter; advised by a number of prominent citizens that observation balloons could play a part in defending the beleaguered republic, the government in the fall of 1793 appropriated funds for a balloon and its support facilities.

The noted chemist Jean Marie-Joseph Coutelle was put in charge of the fledgling aeronautical project. His first mission was hardly a rousing success. Dispatched to the town of Maubeuge, where the French General Jean-Baptiste Jourdan was bracing for an Austrian attack, Coutelle was received skeptically and sent packing back to Paris. "A battalion is needed more at the front than a balloon," sniffed a high official attached to Jourdan's staff.

Returning to the capital, Coutelle conducted several more months of tests, seeking to show that a balloon might be as useful as a battalion. So convincing were his demonstrations that on April 2, 1794, the French authorities formed the world's first air force, known formally as the Compagnie d'Aérostiers and commanded by the freshly commissioned Captain Coutelle. Lest the *aérostiers* be mistaken for mere foot soldiers, the 34 officers and men in the company outfitted themselves in distinctive blue uniforms with black collars and red piping.

The principal mission of Coutelle's balloonists was aerial observation of hostile positions and troop movements. Their duties also were to include relaying signals between friendly forces and sprinkling propaganda leaflets on the heads of the enemy. Coutelle had planned his operations carefully. On observation flights, two men would ascend at a time, one to concentrate on surveillance while the other communicated with the ground by waving signal flags or by stuffing messages into sandbags and sliding them down the long mooring ropes on metal rings. Crewmen on the ground would operate a windlass to pay out the mooring ropes and to haul the balloon down again. The most unwieldy part of the scheme would be the production of hydrogen gas, to be generated from water by passing steam over hot iron particles set in a brick furnace that would be immovable once in place. For the *aérostiers* to keep up with the tides of battle, they would have to haul their balloon, called *L'Entreprenant (The Enterprise),* from place to place while it was still inflated.

The balloonists' first posting was to Maubeuge, where Coutelle had been greeted so coolly the previous fall. They reached the combat zone before their balloon did and soon had the opportunity to convince their doubtful brothers-in-arms that they could fight as well as fly. Ordered into battle against the Austrians, the *aérostiers* acquitted themselves with sufficient honor—losing a junior officer and two enlisted men in the process—to silence the skeptical infantrymen. They rose

Floating unscathed over the battlefield at Fleurus in 1794, French balloon-corps commander Jean Coutelle scouts the movements of the Austrian army while his aide prepares reports, which he will slide down the balloon's tethering lines to French officers who are waiting below.

even higher in the Army's estimation after Coutelle made his first observation flight in early June; an officer of the French general staff was so delighted with the results that he ordered the *aérostiers* to make twice-daily ascents.

Not surprisingly, this enthusiasm was absent on the other side of the lines. Austrian and Dutch officers regarded aerial observation as an unsporting breach of the rules of gentlemanly warfare; their awe-struck foot soldiers believed that *L'Entreprenant* was the work of supernatural powers. In either case, the bulbous intruder did not go unchallenged for long; Austrian artillerymen quickly rigged up the world's first antiaircraft guns by lowering the tailpieces of their cannon into ditches to raise their normal elevation limit.

L'Entreprenant was as safe as careful preparation could make it. The silk envelope had been designed to withstand the pounding winds that tethered balloons must endure and was further fortified by a special varnish that prevented gas leakage. But Coutelle knew that no amount of scientific ingenuity could protect it from a direct hit by a cannon ball; if that happened the gas would spill out of the resultant holes with potentially disastrous results. A few days after the balloon's initial ascent, Coutelle was on observation duty at a dangerously low altitude when a ball from the concealed Austrian battery suddenly whistled over the top of the balloon. Seconds later another shot grazed the gondola. Employing a prudent blend of audacity and self-preservation, the balloonist shouted *"Vive la République"* in the direction of the gunners, while simultaneously signaling his ground crew to let the balloon rise out of range.

This touch of bravado won the *aérostiers* a reputation for the gallant gesture, a characteristic that female French patriots in particular found irresistible. The balloon-borne bravos became the glamor boys of the war, and occasionally they took young women aloft for unauthorized joy rides over the countryside.

At the end of June, Coutelle and his men lugged the fully inflated *L'Entreprenant* from Maubeuge into nearby Belgium, where French forces were attacking the Dutch at Charleroi. Restrained by 20 guide ropes held by husky *aérostiers,* the bulging balloon made the 20-mile journey to its new destination in 15 hours, maneuvering past enemy outposts at an altitude just high enough to permit the passage of cavalrymen who were rushing toward the battle.

The French troops that surrounded Charleroi had heard of *L'Entreprenant's* earlier successful performance at Maubeuge, and they greeted the balloon's arrival with cheers. Coutelle was quick to show that their enthusiasm for aerial observation was well founded. On the day after his arrival, he took a French commander, General Antoine Morlot, aloft; Morlot, peering through his telescope, quickly perceived that the Dutch were badly weakened. Sure enough, the enemy garrison capitulated soon afterward.

The balloonists got a fresh chance to prove their worth a few days

Napoleon's inventive balloon maker

Balloons were largely the product of hit-or-miss engineering until the appointment of French artist-inventor Nicolas-Jacques Conté to head the world's first balloon school and factory at the Château de Meudon in 1794. Building balloons for use in the war against Austria, Conté refined the materials and techniques of their construction—and kept a record of his work in the meticulous watercolors below.

A physicist and chemist as well as an inventive wizard, Conté devised a flexible varnish containing India rubber that did not react with hydrogen and thus reduced leakage. His balloons could remain inflated as long as three months.

Five balloons were built at Meudon, but not without tragedy. Leaking gas exploded in the lab, blinding Conté's left eye. He nevertheless accompanied Napoleon on the Egyptian campaign with a Meudon balloon. Conté's ability to improvise tools, surgical instruments and machines helped sustain the French after the bloody Battle of Abukir.

Napoleon proclaimed Conté a genius "capable of creating the arts of France in the deserts of Arabia." But the praise did not extend to Conté's balloons. Napoleon never used one in battle and in 1799 ordered the factory-school closed.

Meudon cutters trim taffeta into triangular pieces called gores.

Laboratory aides test a new batch of varnish on a taffeta gore.

Inflated in a domed room, a balloon is varnished and sealed.

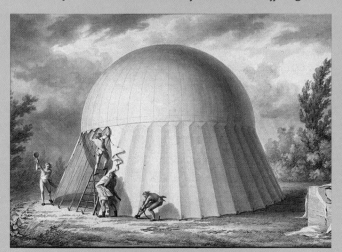

Outdoors, the balloon is finished off with a windbreak skirt.

later when French and Austrian armies clashed at Fleurus, Belgium. Coutelle, accompanied once more by General Morlot, was in the air before the infantrymen below had fired the first shot. The commanders on the ground attached written questions to a cord that Coutelle hauled into the basket while the general fixed his glass on the pageant unfolding some 1,300 feet below.

Never in the history of warfare had men observed the changing tides of battle from such a vantage point. The conflict looked to Coutelle and Morlot like an engagement of toy soldiers. Little puffs of smoke curled up from the artillery, followed a moment later by the flash and thunder of exploding shells. Cavalrymen formed up and galloped into battle as the aerial observers scribbled hurried notes and sent them whizzing down the mooring rope in sandbags. Coutelle wrote later that he could see everything—"the corps of infantry and cavalry, the parks of artillery and their movements, and the massed troops." The two men remained aloft for nearly 10 hours, directing the maneuvers that contributed, at day's end, to a convincing victory for the French. One partisan official was so impressed that he likened an army without a balloon to a blindfolded duelist.

But achievement and praise could not change the essentially fragile nature of this unlikely implement of war. Not long after the victory at Fleurus, while being paraded through the streets of Brussels with the triumphant French Army, L'Entreprenant was ignominiously deflated when its silken body became snagged on a sharp-pointed stake. The accident was an omen of further deflations to come.

The punctured war balloon was patched and ready for duty soon enough, and in 1795 it served the Army well in the Battle of Mayence. But L'Entreprenant and the bold French aérostiers would not taste again the success they had savored on the fields of Fleurus. For the next half decade the balloon service experienced a series of occasional and modest accomplishments interspersed with discouraging mishaps and growing indications of high-level indifference. The government had established a school for balloonists at the Château de Meudon near Paris and three more companies were trained there. But the high command's disenchantment with ballooning was evident in a 1797 dispatch from a general who complained that he could find no use for the aérostiers under his command. In the same year, Napoleon Bonaparte took a balloon company along on his invasion of Egypt, but his enthusiasm for aerial warfare was so tepid that he left the balloon and its gear on board ship when the troops went ashore. Injury piled on insult when the ship bearing the balloon was sunk by the British in the Battle of the Nile.

On his return to France, Napoleon disbanded the aérostiers and closed the balloon school. His disdain for balloons was reinforced by an incident in 1804 during the gala celebration of his coronation as Emperor. The showman André Jacques Garnerin released a hydrogen balloon embellished with a large gilded crown to commemorate the event. The unmanned craft rose majestically into the sky over Paris and

The Napoleonic invasion of England that never came is envisioned as a three-pronged attack—by air, sea and a tunnel beneath the Channel—in this 1803 engraving. The artist, obviously no aeronaut, shows the same wind blowing the French balloons toward the English coast and the defenders' manned kites toward France.

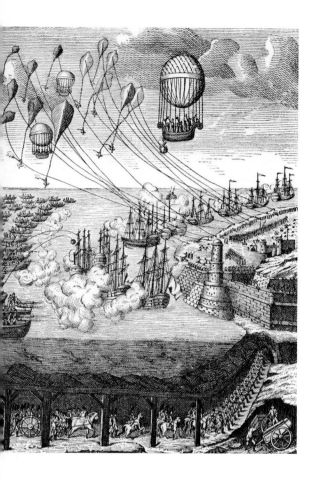

drifted out of sight, only to appear the next day over Rome; it fell at last into Lake Bracciano, but not before depositing a section of the festive crown on the tomb of the ill-starred Roman tyrant Nero. For the superstitious Napoleon, this ominous mishap was proof enough that balloons were not to be trusted.

The generals of the world, retreating into their habitual suspicion of unconventional notions, shared Napoleon's misgivings; for almost the next 50 years they virtually ignored balloons. The promise displayed at Fleurus was shrugged off as an exaggerated fluke. In France, a scheme for an aerial invasion of Britain was dismissed out of hand. England, secure behind its shield of sea power, had little use for war balloons, and a Danish plan to drop bombs and propaganda leaflets from the air came to nothing. Military aeronautics seemed to be an idea whose time had come and gone.

Appropriately enough it was the Austrians, perhaps still smarting from their role as the first victims of military balloons, who revived the idea of aerial warfare—if only briefly. Besieging Venice during the Italian War for Independence in 1849, the Austrians armed a flotilla of unmanned hot-air balloons with bombs fitted with time fuses. This pioneer bombing mission was launched on a favorable wind, but the luckless Austrians then stared in dismay as a shift in wind direction sent many of the balloons drifting back over their own lines. Damage on either side was negligible. The episode was followed by yet another long standstill in European military ballooning; 21 years would pass before another serious venture was attempted, and then it would have an entirely new purpose, as balloons became the precarious communications life line for a besieged capital. In the meantime, the focus of war ballooning crossed the Atlantic to a sundered America.

The United States that was rocked by the outbreak of civil war in April of 1861 was a nation infatuated with balloon flight. The exploits of such balloonists as John Wise, John LaMountain and Thaddeus Lowe had been front-page news for years. Reporters had written breathtaking accounts of the ordeal endured by Wise and LaMountain in their storm-hounded voyage across Lake Ontario in 1859; LaMountain had made the headlines again in that year when he suffered through four days in the Canadian wilderness after his balloon went astray.

Thaddeus Sobieski Constantine Lowe, part showman and part serious balloonist, combined a talent for promotion with his aeronautical skills. Born in New Hampshire in 1832 (his mother, an avid reader, is believed to have named him for a fictional Polish hero), Lowe exhibited a boyhood curiosity about aeronautics, sometimes using kites to send aloft the family cat. By 1854, having worked for a time as an assistant to a traveling magician, Lowe had decided on a career in ballooning. After four years of study he built his first balloon; he soon gained a reputation as an accomplished aeronaut. His well-trumpeted plan to cross the Atlantic by balloon, though it failed, made him a national figure. And his unplanned touchdown in the heart of secessionist South Carolina on a pre-Atlantic test flight in the spring of 1861 left him thinking about how balloons might serve the Union in the growing conflict between North and South.

Balloons had never been deployed by an American army, though their use had been suggested—and spurned—at least twice before. In 1840, after United States troops had tried in vain for five years to put down the rebellious Seminole Indians of Florida, an imaginative Army colonel suggested that balloon reconnaissance could help locate hidden enemy encampments. Two years later, when the Florida Indian wars finally drew to a close, the aerial-observation scheme was still tied down by military red tape.

Not long after the outbreak of the Mexican War in 1846, John Wise had come up with his own proposal for military aeronautics. Wise's widely publicized plan called for the bombardment from a manned balloon of the powerful fortress of San Juan de Ulúa in the strategic Mexican port city of Veracruz. One commentator noted that it would be a "very troublesome matter to enlist the volunteers" to lob bombshells from Wise's proposed altitude of 5,000 feet. The proposal failed to get the endorsement of the U.S. War Department.

By the time of the Civil War, the high command was generally more receptive to the idea of aeronautics. Nevertheless, the Union Army's balloon operations got off to a chaotic start. The patriotic aeronauts who rushed to volunteer as balloon observers had to make their own arrangements with individual officers; unlike the 18th Century French *aérostiers,* the American military balloonists retained their civilian status. Their equipment, for the most part, was not well suited to the stresses of tethered flight, and most of the officers and soldiers with whom they served lacked even the most elemental understanding of the special requirements and frailties of balloons.

In June and July 1861, with Confederate troops massing at Bull Run, southwest of Washington, no fewer than four balloonists were seeking acceptance as Union aeronauts. James Allen, attached to the Rhode Island regiment led by Colonel Ambrose Burnside, performed a successful demonstration flight in the capital, but then saw his hopes for action dashed when his inflated balloon was destroyed in an encounter with a telegraph pole while en route to the front. John LaMountain, who had offered his services at the outbreak of hostilities only to be ignored, was then summoned to conduct aerial observations at Fortress Monroe, a key Union outpost near the mouth of the James River in Virginia. The 53-year-old John Wise, who had first volunteered for front-line combat duty, was ordered to build a balloon and bring it to Washington, where he was quickly mired in the bureaucratic turmoil that beset the wartime capital.

Only the adroit Thaddeus Lowe was able to thread his way successfully through the administrative minefields of Washington, and even he had his share of problems. Lowe's acquaintance with Secretary Joseph

"Will Lieut. Genl. Scott please see Professor Lowe once more about his balloon?" wrote President Lincoln in July 1861. Scott refused, until Lincoln personally escorted Lowe to Army headquarters. Later, armed with a spyglass (top), Lowe went off to scout the Confederates.

The old steamer George Washington Parke Custis becomes a mobile launching site for Lowe's ascents along the Potomac. The ship's resemblance to the Union's ironclad Monitor was a deterrent to enemy attack, Lowe wrote, "for the Monitor was what the Confederates dreaded."

Henry of the Smithsonian Institution and the warm support of Treasury Secretary Salmon Chase landed him a meeting with Abraham Lincoln. The President listened with interest as Lowe outlined a plan for a corps of balloonists who would communicate with the ground by telegraph. The War Department promptly authorized funds to enable Lowe to make a trial ascent from the mall between the Capitol and the unfinished Washington Monument in a balloon named, like the original French war balloon of the 1790s, *Enterprise*. On June 18, 1861, Lowe and two representatives of the telegraph company rose to an altitude of about 500 feet, from which point they could see for nearly 25 miles in every direction. Lowe dictated a message to President Lincoln: "The city with its girdle of encampments presents a superb scene," he said. "I have pleasure in sending you this first dispatch ever telegraphed from an aerial station."

In late June, Lowe made several tethered ascents from the Union lines outside of Washington, but his position with the Army was complicated somewhat by the continued presence of Wise. The latter had

As Union soldiers man gas generators, Thaddeus Lowe (right rear) feels his balloon fill in this Mathew Brady photo taken at Fair Oaks, Virginia.

promised to build a balloon for some $200 less than Lowe and thus had received the government's first balloon contract; Lowe, in order to remain in contention as a potential military balloonist, had to content himself with refurbishing the old *Enterprise* at his own expense. Indeed, during the hectic days of preparation for the first Battle of Bull Run in July, Lowe on one occasion was forced to yield his position at a city gas main while Wise inflated his own balloon with the coal gas that was frequently substituted for hydrogen. Unhappily for the Union cause, Wise's craft was ripped by tree branches on its way to Bull Run and saw no action. (Upbraided by an officer for his failure to take to the air during the Union defeat that ensued, Wise remarked wryly: "The balloon part was just about as good as the fighting part.")

Lowe, learning of Wise's undoing, had hurriedly inflated his own balloon, but he was too late: As he rushed toward the scene of battle he was met by a stream of retreating Union soldiers. A few days later Lowe atoned for his tardiness by making a free flight over the Confederate positions near Washington, returning to Union territory on a high-altitude air current. It was almost his last trip. Friendly troops, mistaking the approaching *Enterprise* for a Confederate craft, opened fire on it, and Lowe had to float on until he was out of range. Once back on the ground, he assured anxious Washingtonians that they were in no danger of attack; he also asked the War Department to inform trigger-happy soldiers that all "air vessels seen thus far, and probably that will be seen hereafter, are for Union purposes."

Not everyone in the Union high command agreed that balloons could serve a useful purpose. General Winfield Scott, the crusty 75-year-old head of the Army, believed balloons to be "of little use" in military operations, and Scott's objections were all that stood between Lowe and permanent designation as an Army aeronaut. Two days after his nearly tragic free flight in the *Enterprise,* the young balloonist sought out the commanding general to plead his case.

Armed with a handwritten note from the President himself, Lowe went to Scott's Washington headquarters, where an orderly informed him that the general was much too busy to see him. A few hours later he tried again, with the same result. On a third visit he was told that Scott was dining; still later he was advised that the general was asleep. Boiling with indignation, Lowe stormed back to the White House and again appealed to the President for help. Lincoln straightaway donned his stovepipe hat and escorted the frustrated aeronaut to Scott's headquarters, where they were received with promptness and courtesy. One week later Lowe was installed as a regular Union balloonist—at a generous wage of $10 per day—and he was authorized to construct a reconnaissance balloon at the government's expense.

While Lowe was persevering in Washington, the theatrical John La-Mountain was grabbing most of the early glory in the field. Ascending to 1,400 feet over Fortress Monroe on July 31, he spied out a hidden Confederate camp; three days later he lifted off from the deck of the Union transport *Fanny,* which thus qualified as the world's first aircraft carrier. LaMountain filed detailed reports after these missions, and drew diagrams showing the enemy's strength and position. "On the left bank of James River about eight or nine miles from Newport News," he said in one dispatch, "is a large encampment of the enemy, from 150 to 200 tents." Along with the balloon's surveillance value to the Union, the mere sight of it bobbing above their encampments unsettled the Confederates. A Northern newspaperman, after interviewing a runaway slave, reported that the Southerners' "rage amounted to a perfect frenzy. Nothing else has occurred which has so much enraged them."

Their fury would be short-lived. LaMountain's operations were dependent on his supply of hydrogen gas, which ran out after two weeks. Fortress Monroe's commander, delighted with the aeronaut's work, granted his request to return home to Troy, New York, for a larger balloon and a new gas generator. But when LaMountain reported back to the fort he found a new commander who had little interest in either ballooning or balloonists. Transferred to the Army of the Potomac, which was serving along the stalemated front in northern Virginia, LaMountain made a number of daring free flights. But a chronic inability to share the limelight now put him on an inevitable collision course with Thaddeus Lowe.

Lowe had been quietly consolidating his position as the Union's premier aeronaut, an enterprise that was greatly simplified in August by the departure of the frustrated James Allen and John Wise from Army service. He scored a major breakthrough at Fort Corcoran, Virginia, in September when he directed artillery fire from his airborne perch by telegraphing his observations to the gunners below. Lowe's regular reconnaissance flights also diverted the Confederates to time-consuming efforts at camouflage and deception, most notably the construction of dummy artillery pieces, called "Quaker guns," out of logs and stovepipes. Lowe was clearly rendering yeoman service to his country, and his rising star acquired still more luster when he aroused the interest of General George McClellan, who in November of 1861 replaced Scott as comander of the Union forces.

The patronage of McClellan, who rode with Lowe on several tethered ascents, brought Lowe what he had wanted all along: the authority to build more balloons and to recruit a corps of civilian balloonists. Despite this expansion, it soon became plain that the corps was not big enough to hold both Lowe and LaMountain. Lowe regarded LaMountain's well-publicized free flights as showmanship unredeemed by military value; LaMountain in turn resented McClellan's order that he serve under Lowe. A fusillade of name calling ended with LaMountain's dismissal from Army service in February 1862.

Lowe, his position secured, took advantage of the winter lull in the fighting to oversee the construction of six new balloons, stitched by sure-fingered seamstresses. The balloons, each supplied with a mobile hydrogen generator of Lowe's design, along with the requisite rigging, telegraph cable and other equipment, were given suitably patriotic names—*Constitution, Washington, United States*—and ornamented with elaborate decorations. Lowe also assembled a cadre of aeronauts, including the previously disaffected James Allen and an experienced German-born balloonist, John Steiner. In the spring, Lowe was ordered to join McClellan's army as chief aeronaut in its projected march up the James River to the Confederate capital at Richmond. By this time Lowe had strung out his squadron of balloons in a line that stretched from Union-occupied Port Royal, South Carolina, to the Mississippi River.

The performance of Lowe's balloons was one of the few cheering developments during McClellan's unsuccessful bid to seize Richmond.

As his ground crew pays out the tethering lines, Thaddeus Lowe rises to reconnoiter the battlefield at Fair Oaks, Virginia, in 1862. His gondola was emblazoned with stars and stripes so that Union troops would not fire on him by mistake.

Indeed, at the battle of Fair Oaks, on May 31 and June 1, 1862, Lowe's aerial observations probably staved off a crushing Union defeat.

The first day of battle found Lowe on board the *Washington,* hovering high above the front lines and scanning the horizon for signs of enemy movement. He soon spotted a large concentration of Confederate troops massing for the attack. On the ground, some Union commanders judged that the Southern forces were merely staging a feint, but Lowe could clearly see that an all-out assault was on the way; the telegraphed warnings tapped out from his balloon alerted headquarters in time to dispatch reinforcements to hold the line.

On the following day, Lowe went aloft in the *Washington* once more. Seeing that a major engagement was about to begin, he returned quickly to the ground, intending to switch to the larger balloon *Intrepid* and ascend to higher altitudes, where he would have a better view of the action below. He commandeered a horse and galloped the six miles to his balloon base, but his mobile gas-generating equipment was not up to inflating the *Intrepid* as rapidly as the needs of battle required. When the balloon was just half-filled, Lowe calculated that it would take at least another hour before it was airworthy—by then, he knew, the Union lines might well be overwhelmed by regiments of advancing Southerners.

Desperate now to be aloft, Lowe hustled his telegraph equipment into the gondola of a third balloon, the smaller *Constitution,* and cast off, only to find that it, too, lacked the lifting power to rise. "I saw the two armies coming nearer and nearer together," Lowe wrote later. "There was no time to be lost." It occurred to him that it might be possible to transfer gas from the inadequate *Constitution* to the half-filled *Intrepid,* thus saving an hour that "would be worth a million dollars a minute."

The problem was that Lowe had no equipment to make such a transfer—until he spotted a 10-inch cooking pot sitting nearby. Ordering a soldier to cut the bottom from the pot, Lowe used the remaining portion as a crude pipe to connect the two balloons. The *Intrepid* was quickly inflated with gas transferred from the *Constitution;* Lowe and his telegraph operator at last rose far above the battle, and soon were "keeping the wires hot with information." At one point during the fighting, Lowe was instructed to dispatch progress reports at 15-minute intervals; these observations were then relayed to Washington and a worried President Lincoln, who was especially gratified when Lowe finally reported that the Confederate forces had turned back toward Richmond.

Lowe's fellow balloonists were given few opportunities to perform such critical missions. John Starkweather, assigned to Port Royal, South Carolina, was reduced to despair by his cold reception. "I have not had any orders from the general," he wrote to Lowe. "You say you are anxious that every member of the Aeronautic Department should render all the valuable service possible. I am anxious to do the same. All I want is the chance." Aeronaut John Steiner met even more resistance on the Mississippi. The officers, he reported in his precarious English, "say thay know nothing about my balloon business and thay even laugh ad me. Give me a paper from Headvaurters to show theas blockheads hoo I am."

The South, handicapped by a Union blockade that severely limited the availability of necessary material, was never able to mount a serious challenge in the air. A plucky captain named John Randolph Bryan, innocent of any aerial experience, made a few tentative forays in a cotton hot-air balloon in the spring of 1862. But Captain Bryan's aerial adventures were suspended soon after a well-meaning comrade—seeking to aid another soldier whose leg had become ensnarled by the balloon's mooring cable—cut the cable and set Bryan adrift on an involuntary free flight. The Confederates next fielded a gas balloon patched together from sheets of different-colored silk, giving rise to the charming legend of a "silk dress" balloon fashioned from the clothing of patriotic daughters of the Confederacy. This balloon enjoyed a brief career before it was captured by Union troops when the boat transporting it went aground. The final Confederate entry, another vision in multihued silk, suffered a similar fate: Snatched from the ground by a strong gust, it was deposited in Union territory, where it became a prisoner of war.

Lowe's command too became a casualty of the War. The collapse of McClellan's drive on Richmond and a subsequent change in the Union high command in mid-1862 robbed the Union's top balloonist of his most important military champion. The bureaucratic ineptitude that had beset the balloon corps from the beginning—commands that overlapped, transport vehicles that never arrived, paychecks that appeared with galling infrequency—grew steadily worse. Most disheartening of all was the inactivity: Lowe had to wait from June until December before he was once again ordered into action, this time at Fredericksburg. But he played only a minor role in the battle. It was May 1863 before the Army of the Potomac saw serious action again, in the Battle of Chancellorsville. Lowe made several ascents during this engagement and relayed valuable intelligence to General Joseph Hooker's headquarters, but they would be his last flights for the Union.

For the proud and ambitious Lowe, the final insult was the appointment of an officer named Cyrus Comstock as his immediate superior. Lowe was accustomed to a certain free-wheeling latitude in his dealings with the military, but Comstock was a traditionalist who insisted that the balloonist operate through proper military channels and reprimanded him when he failed to do so. Then Comstock cut Lowe's pay from $10 to $6 per day and ordered him to dismiss his father, who had been working with the ground crew. On May 7, nearly two years after his triumphant demonstration flight in Washington, Lowe resigned from the Army. In late June, as the Army of the Potomac marched toward Gettysburg, the balloon corps was officially dissolved.

Thirty-five years would pass before an American balloon was again

Inflating in the Place Saint-Pierre, the balloon Neptune is prepared for departure from besieged Paris in September 1870 with pilot Jules Duruof and 200 pounds of government dispatches and civilian mail.

used in battle. But the performance of balloons in the Civil War had convinced a number of foreign observers that lighter-than-air vehicles had a definite role to play in modern warfare. Appropriately enough, balloons were next used for military purposes in France, where the first *aérostiers* had taken to the air in the closing decade of the 18th Century.

The scene at Paris' Place Saint-Pierre in September 1870 was like a caricature of those resplendent moments when ballooning was in its colorful infancy. The bold and confident aeronaut climbed into his frail gondola; the balloon swayed gently on its ropes. The murmur of the crowd rose to a full-throated roar as the balloonist cast off ballast and his vessel leaped from the pavement to the morning sky, arching above the placid River Seine. Aeronaut Jules Duruof peered over the side at the brilliant city diminishing before his eyes. It was just like the early days.

But Duruof's balloon was no gaily painted confection; it was an old and leaky veteran. And the mission that sent him sailing soundlessly over the countryside beyond Paris was no triumphant demonstration of a new wonder but an act of deliverance: Duruof was escaping a city under siege. The angry cannons of the Prussians sent ineffectual bursts

The hopes of embattled Paris ride with Interior Minister Léon Gambetta (in fur hat, beside gondola at left) as he prepares to take off by balloon from Montmartre on October 7, 1870. Gambetta arrived in Tours safely and took over the French national defense effort.

of fire at him as he drifted across their siege lines and coolly showered visiting cards—his only means of retaliation—on their heads. Duruof's cargo was 227 pounds of mail, the first to leave Paris since the siege had begun a few days before. He also carried the hopes of Parisians that balloons would somehow help them survive. With every means of ground communication cut off, balloons represented the only link between Paris and the outside world—including France's provisional government in Tours, 125 miles to the southwest.

The notion of using balloons as a life line for the besieged was as old as ballooning itself, but the French were about to test the idea on a scale never before imagined. Before this extraordinary effort ended, the country would build a fleet of balloons and train the men to fly them; the essential business of a nation at war would be transacted through messages carried by balloon; divided families would remain in touch, and a flock of carrier pigeons would be assembled to bring word from the outside back to the city. In the end a total of 66 balloons carrying 102 passengers and two and a half million letters left Paris in this way, and all but eight of the balloons landed safely and among friends.

On the first such flight, Jules Duruof returned peacefully to earth on the grounds of a château about 50 miles west of the capital. Government dispatches in hand, he boarded a train to carry them personally to Tours. Other aeronauts took two more flights in the next week, carrying a dozen pigeons for use in bearing messages back to Paris. These flights also reduced the city's supply of serviceable balloons to one, which was assigned to the well-known balloonist Gaston Tissandier. He ascended on the last day of September with three pigeons and 25,000 letters, although his first good look at the balloon that day almost drained away his nerve: There were "holes big enough for my little finger to pass through," he wailed, "a whole constellation of punctures. This is no longer a balloon, it is a skimmer."

Overcoming his doubts that he could clear even the treetops, Tissandier rose above the Prussian guns to an altitude of 3,000 feet and floated toward Versailles. The novel sight of his battle-scarred homeland spread out beneath him was "sad, barren, horrible," the balloonist wrote later. "Not a soul on the roads, not a carriage, not a train," he recalled. "All the demolished bridges offer the appearance of abandoned ruins. Not a soldier, not a sentinel, nothing. You might think yourself on the outskirts of an ancient city destroyed by time."

Trouble soon jolted Tissandier out of his gloomy reverie. Forced downward by cooling temperatures that contracted the gas in his balloon, he came perilously close to a troop of Prussian cavalrymen. But Tissandier managed to fling out enough ballast—and bundles of anti-Prussian propaganda—to rise again out of range. Two hours later he made a bracing but relatively painless landing when a sudden downdraft seized his balloon at an altitude of 50 feet and pushed it to earth. Like Duruof, Tissandier traveled on to Tours by rail.

In Paris, meanwhile, a force of seamstresses, workmen and land-

Scouting the battle from on high

During the three decades before World War I, military observation balloons became part of the panorama of battle in the wars and revolutions that flickered across the world, from Cuba to Casablanca to Capetown and from Manchuria to Southeast Asia.

In 1884 balloons were instrumental in helping a French expeditionary force in Indochina to capture the strategic town of Dienbienphu. During the Russo-Japanese War, the materials that were dispatched to build Russian balloons in Manchuria were captured by the Japanese, who already had an efficient balloon corps of their own—modeled on German technology. In desperation, a Czarist officer devised a balloon of bed sheets coated with flax oil.

In the Boer War of 1899-1902, teams of British balloonists were used to spot hidden Boer positions and call in artillery, including the Long Toms brought ashore by a Royal Navy brigade. But this kind of duty was dangerous and—according to balloon-corps commander P. W. L. Broke-Smith—some English wives, fearing for the safety of their menfolk, conspired to keep them too heavy for acceptance by the balloon school at Aldershot by giving them "the time of their lives in the matter of feeding."

In the Spanish-American War, a U.S. balloon surveys the assault on Santiago de Cuba. The balloon lasted one day in combat.

A balloon section, including wagons carrying hydrogen tubes, accompanies the British Army to Johannesburg in the Boer War.

Braving searchlights that could focus artillery on them, Japanese spotters observe Russian defenses at Port Arthur, Manchuria, in 1904.

A French balloon unit fords the Neffifigh River on its way to scout Muslim rebels during the Moroccan campaign of 1907-1908.

locked sailors, who were supervised by the veteran balloonist Eugène Godard, worked tirelessly to replenish the supply of balloons that Tissandier's flight had exhausted. Two huge railroad stations had been transformed into temporary balloon factories; the British journalist Henry Vizetelly described the bizarre and bustling scene at one of them, the Gare d'Orléans:

"Under the vast iron and glass arched roof—on the long metal rafters of which sailors balanced themselves or sat astride, engaged in suspending long strips of colored calico reaching almost to the ground, scores of women were occupied, either in spreading out and ironing long pieces of material or else in soaking the calico to get rid of its stiffness. Having been hung up to dry, the material was then cut out to the various patterns, marked out to their full size upon the ground, and after a preliminary varnishing a hundred or more work-girls, seated at long tables and superintended by Madame Godard, proceeded to sew the seams with a mechanical exactitude." Each balloon, which took about 12 days to complete, was equipped with a wicker car, a small pigeon cage and the necessary barometer—for gauging altitude—compass and thermometer.

Thousands of Parisians flocked to the Place Saint-Pierre on October 7, 1870, to cheer the ascent of one of the first of the new balloons. Its passenger, snug in a long greatcoat and fur hat, was the most important traveler who would ride a siege balloon—Minister of the Interior Léon Gambetta, whose mission was to reinvigorate the faltering government in Tours and to organize and rally an army. He almost missed his chance. Dropping uncomfortably low over a Prussian-held area, his balloon escaped capture only when the pilot hastily jettisoned ballast. An enemy bullet grazed Gambetta's hand as the craft soared out of range and leveled off at an altitude so high that the earth looked to the shaken Minister like "a badly designed carpet."

The landing near Montdidier, 55 miles north of Paris, was another near-miss: The basket snagged in the branches of a large oak tree and overturned, nearly dumping its occupants. Local peasants rescued Gambetta, and a pigeon was sent homing back to Paris with the eagerly awaited news that he had landed safely and was proceeding to Tours.

The balloon flights persisted through October and into November, as the Prussian vise on Paris gradually tightened. Prussian artillery continued to pound the city. French authorities, alarmed by reports of a new enemy antiballoon gun, which was mounted on a swivel, decreed in late November that all subsequent balloon ascensions would take place under cover of night. This change led to the most extraordinary flight of the siege. Two aeronauts, flying in darkness and uncertain of their location, went on a 15-hour, 800-mile voyage across the North Sea; when they finally landed they found themselves, to their astonishment, in the snow-carpeted wilds of central Norway. The men were bearing a vital communiqué informing Gambetta and his commanders of a plan

Germans parade their sausage-shaped observation balloons during World War I. Germany produced 1,870 such balloons during the War and lost 655 to enemy planes and artillery and to bad weather.

to break through the siege. By the time the weary balloonists had made their way by land to Oslo, and from there to Tours, the breakout attempt was already under way. It failed, and so in the end did Gambetta's gallant effort to organize French resistance.

The 66th and final flight of the siege took off on January 28, 1871, the same day that an armistice ending the Franco-Prussian War was signed at Versailles. A month later Prussian troops paraded through Paris. And soon after that the French showed that they had learned at least one valuable lesson from the siege: The ballooning school that Napoleon had closed more than 70 years before was reopened.

The dramatic success of the Paris airlift, combined with American aeronauts' achievements in the Civil War, had forcefully demonstrated the two great military functions that balloons were equipped to perform—battlefield reconnaissance and communication under siege. In Europe, at least, the French and American successes had erased the upper-echelon skepticism that had clouded military ballooning since

Napoleon's day. One by one the great powers of the late 19th Century—Great Britain, Germany, Russia, Austria-Hungary—blossomed forth with military aerostats and *aérostiers* of their own. New schools were established; captive balloons accompanied the troops on their maneuvers. The British contributed an important refinement in 1884 by developing portable cylinders for the storage of compressed hydrogen; the cylinders were a significant improvement on the cumbersome traveling generators that Lowe had used.

Embracing military ballooning with the ardor of a belated convert, the British sent observers aloft during colonial forays in China, Egypt and Bechuanaland and fielded no fewer than four balloon sections during the Boer War of 1899-1902. In America too military enthusiasm for ballooning revived in the 1890s, though the performance of the solitary balloon that was ordered into action at San Juan Hill during the Spanish-American War was less than inspiring. Launched too close to the Spanish lines, the balloon *Santiago* was riddled with so many bullet holes that it was obliged to retire from the field of battle after less than a day of combat.

Sharing his gondola with the outsized lens of an aerial reconnaissance camera, a German balloonist is ready to go aloft on the Western Front in World War I. Tethered balloons, which were more stable than airplanes, made excellent platforms for aerial photography.

As balloons grew more popular with the military, the graceful spherical shape that had characterized them through their first century was recognized as a liability. The traditional globular balloon was ideal for free flight, but it could rotate wildly when anchored to the ground; a violent gust could easily flip its lightweight basket parallel to the earth. To solve these problems, the military aeronauts of the late 19th Century developed an egg-shaped craft designed to nose diagonally into the wind—in effect a tethered dirigible without an engine. The Germans launched the first of these relatively stable kite balloons (known to the Germans as "dragons" and to the Allies as "sausages") in 1896.

Within 20 years the new balloons would be in general use in the first of two great world wars. By then the French had designed a more streamlined kite balloon, named Caquot for its inventor, which could operate in even stronger winds and at higher altitudes. The craft was large enough to support two gondolas, and three large stabilizing fins at its stern gave it something of the appearance of a Disneyesque elephant. All the major contending armies—German, French, British and American—employed squadrons of these balloons on the Western Front for artillery spotting and general observation.

Though their equipment was more sophisticated, the balloonists of World War I had the same mission as the earliest *aérostiers*. Armed with maps, binoculars, a telephone linked to gunners on the ground and a parachute—but no weapons—the balloon observers were released by winches to elevations as high as 6,000 feet. Once aloft, they trained their glasses on enemy positions, coordinated their observations with maps and alerted the artillerymen below.

But the modern aeronaut no longer enjoyed the virtual immunity from enemy fire that had blessed his earlier brethren. The immobile, hydrogen-filled "sausages" were tempting targets for newly developed antiaircraft guns; they were also appetizing prey for swift, well-armed fighter planes, the balloons' new companions in the sky. Daring pilots on both sides won reputations as "balloon busters" by challenging the concentration of antiaircraft batteries that frequently guarded the vulnerable balloons. Few sights were more terrifying to a balloonist than the approach of enemy planes, their chattering guns spraying the highly flammable balloon bag with bright trails of tracer bullets intended to puncture the balloon and set it afire.

A balloonist faced with such an attack rarely had the means to fight back. The flammable hydrogen gas used to inflate balloons made the use of firearms in the observer's basket foolhardy in the extreme. In any case, gunfire from a stationary balloon would have been a poor defense against a highly maneuverable fighter plane. The balloonist's best response when he was under fire was to use his parachute—almost alone among World War I airmen, he was allowed to wear one—and hope that bits of the blazing balloon did not drift down and burn his lifesaving silk canopy.

Such emergency measures were by no means uncommon. In one

15-day period during the Meuse-Argonne offensive of 1918, American balloonists made 30 parachute jumps while losing 21 balloons—15 of them to German fighter aircraft, six to ground fire. If they landed safely, the steel-nerved observers frequently went up again the same day.

Just as fighter pilots were ranked by the number of enemies they shot down, balloonists earned a kind of reverse recognition for the number of shoot-downs they survived. Lieutenant Glenn Phelps, the unofficial American balloon ace of the War, had to jump for his life five times—all in the space of about four months.

The first of these adventures occurred on July 15, 1918, while Phelps and Lieutenant R. K. Patterson were directing ground fire from an altitude of about 3,500 feet. Artillery rounds began bursting nearby; as they came closer the two men bailed out. Not until they were back on the ground did the two observers learn that the artillery bursts had not been enemy fire after all; they had come from friendly gunners seeking to drive off three enemy aircraft. Half an hour later Phelps and Patterson were in the air once more.

A few hours later, after a long day of relaying information to the ground batteries, the two observers saw five planes droning toward them from their own lines. This time the balloonists assumed they were friendly and discovered otherwise only when staccato bursts of machine-gun fire sprayed the balloon and its basket with incendiary bullets. Both men promptly dived over the edge of the basket. As Phelps descended, the empty basket plummeted past him with blazing shreds of balloon fabric trailing in its wake.

Three weeks later Phelps was attacked once more, this time by a force of no fewer than 11 German fighters. His balloon enveloped in flames, Phelps made his third jump. In late October he leaped again when his balloon was set upon by a single enemy plane; the balloon did not catch fire, and Phelps was preparing to go up in it again when he discovered that the fabric had been perforated with more than 100 bullet holes. Then on November 10, 1918, came Phelps's most exasperating moment: His balloon was attacked and burned by two American pilots who had mistaken it for a German observation craft. Once more, he parachuted and landed safely on the ground. It was his last jump. The following day the War was over, and a British Army communiqué noted: "All along the Front, the balloons are down."

Balloons would rise again in future conflicts, but not with men on board. Already the airplane, armed and mobile, had proved its greater flexibility on observation missions. A ponderous stationary balloon had no role to play in the fluid frontline conditions of modern war, though unmanned balloons would see service as a defense against aircraft—both on land and at sea—during World War II (pages 102-107).

That war also marked the last attempt at aerial bombardment by balloon. Starting in November 1944, the Japanese launched more than 9,000 bomb-bearing balloons toward the United States mainland,

World War I balloonists were told to "drop out" quickly in case of attack, and in this drawing, entitled A Leap for Life, an Allied observer in parachute harness heeds the advice. As he jumps, his weight will pull the chute from its aluminum pack on the outside of the gondola.

Fire, the constant dread of balloonists, engulfs a United States Army hydrogen balloon at Fort Sill, Oklahoma, in 1918, sending soldiers running pell-mell for safety. A spark caused by friction as the bag was deflated started the blaze.

seeking to ignite forest fires and inflict random civilian casualties. The Japanese balloons, code-named "Windship Weapon," were made of sturdy paper or silk and measured some 33 feet in diameter. They were designed to ride the transpacific jet stream to their intended targets, where the bomb loads would be dropped by time fuses. To keep the unmanned balloons at the desired altitude during the three-day, 6,000-mile crossing from Japan to North America, the Japanese designed an ingenious mechanism that discharged ballast automatically when the craft dropped below the jet stream and vented gas when it rose too high.

Most of the silent bombers seem to have dropped into the sea, but at least 285 reached the United States, Canada or Mexico by the time the flights were halted in April 1945. The next month, a woman and five children on an outing near Bly, Oregon, found one of the downed balloons and accidentally triggered its bomb. All of them were killed. Marking the spot today is a plaque that names the victims and commemorates the site as "the only place on the American continent where death resulted from enemy action during World War II." ∿

The silent sentinels

"Barrage Balloons," reported an American journalist from embattled London in the dark days of 1940, "are certainly the most distinctive feature of the view from a city window practically anywhere in Britain today." Indeed, scenes like the one at right, taken near the Houses of Parliament, were commonplace in England—and occasionally on the coasts of the United States—throughout World War II. Like schools of goldfish, clusters of unmanned barrage balloons floated above British cities and towns, factories and power plants, ports and convoys at sea, forming an umbrella against air attack.

The balloons themselves, which were made of rubberized cotton and ranged up to 70,000 cubic feet in size, posed little threat to marauding aircraft. But the strong steel cables that anchored them were another matter. The cables could slice through the wing of an airplane, said one British balloon crewman, "like a grocer's wire goes through cheese." In the first 18 months of the War— through the peak of the Blitz—102 planes collided with balloon cables over Britain, causing 66 confirmed crashes or forced landings. Countless other planes were forced to drop their bombs from above the balloon picket line, which ranged up to 20,000 feet.

Barrage balloons were hailed as "ramparts of the air" and as key girders in the vaunted "roof over Britain." The most eloquent tribute to them, however, may have been the half-serious remark made by one member of an all-female balloon crew in London. "If you cut the balloons loose," she said, "England would sink."

A guardian balloon hovers over the Palace of Westminster during the Battle of Britain in 1940. Balloons were positioned at irregular intervals and altitudes so that unwary attackers were more likely to run afoul of their anchoring cables.

Balloons hover protectively above South African troops at Castellamare, Italy, as they board transports bound for the Anzio beachhead in 1944.

A skyful of balloons tethered to ships and barges screens the Allied invasion convoy as it steams toward Normandy on D-Day, June 6, 1944.

4

Lifting science toward the edge of space

In the summer of 1947, an American businessman in Idaho reported seeing a shiny, disklike object flash across the sky. It was the beginning of a nationwide phenomenon. Soon citizens from coast to coast were reporting similar flights of what came to be called flying saucers. There was wide speculation that the mysterious craft were piloted by beings from other planets.

To this day, the existence and source of unidentified flying objects remains a subject of popular argument, but many of the UFOs of 1947 were in fact high-flying balloons, launched by United States Navy scientists who were working on a secret research project. Measuring some 100 feet high, the unmanned balloons could rise to heights of close to 20 miles; riding the strong winds prevalent at such altitudes, they frequently reached speeds of up to 200 miles per hour. When they were illuminated by light rays and viewed from below, they looked like saucers flitting through the sky.

The Navy's program had an ambitious purpose: to study the nature of cosmic rays, small nuclear particles that bombard the earth's atmosphere from outer space. For if World War II had been the last hurrah for observation and barrage balloons, the balloon was still a valuable tool for scientific research. And although balloons in the mid-20th Century rose far higher—and carried far more sophisticated equipment—than their earlier counterparts, their scientific mission had remained basically unchanged since the first faltering attempts at aerial research. That mission had been defined by one of the pioneer aeronauts in 1784, only a year after the first public ascent of a balloon. Lighter-than-air flight, he said, could lead to "a full investigation of the nature and properties of the atmosphere which surrounds us, and into which we had hitherto been unable to rise."

The man who thus gave balloons their first scientific goal was Dr. John Jeffries, the American expatriate who made the celebrated first balloon crossing of the English Channel with the French aeronaut Jean Pierre Blanchard. Fittingly, Jeffries was also the first to make an ascent for the express purpose of conducting research in the upper air—the earliest of a long procession of scientists who looked upon balloons not as wonders in themselves but as mobile laboratories for the investigation of the unknown.

To such men, the regions above the earth teemed with questions whose answers promised to be of great benefit to mankind. What fac-

A chain of polystyrene weather balloons 1,400 feet long lifts an enclosed gondola bearing French astronomer Audouin Dollfus toward the stratosphere in 1959. Reduced distortion in the thin upper atmosphere allowed Dollfus a clearer view of Venus than was possible from the ground, thus providing a modern example of the balloon's historic worth as a tool of science.

tors determined temperature and humidity, wind speed and direction? How were clouds formed? What was the nature of atmospheric electricity—and how might it be harnessed? How high was it possible for men to rise above the earth? Explorers in the late 19th Century turned to balloons for help in their frustrated attempts to reach the North Pole; scientists of a later generation lofted balloons to penetrate the forbidding stratosphere, a bold first step in man's probe into the planetary system and the universe beyond.

Enduring danger, discomfort and occasional disorientation, the scientist-balloonists pursued their goals with a persistence that was often heroic. Voyaging beyond the limits of human endurance, balloonists died for science long before they ever perished in warfare. The honor roll of fallen aeronauts includes brave men of many nationalities— among them the Frenchmen Joseph Crocé-Spinelli and Théodore Sivel, the Swedish polar explorers Salomon August Andrée, Nils Strindberg and Knut Fraenkel and the American Hawthorne C. Gray. But James Glaisher of England, who barely survived one of the most perilous flights of the 19th Century, expressed the creed of most of his kind

Combining science and spectacle, French aeronaut Pierre Téstu-Brissy ascends on horseback in 1798. Both horse and man survived the test, though Téstu-Brissy discovered that the horse began to bleed from the nose at relatively low altitudes.

when he wrote that one important scientific observation was "worth far more than the risk I have run."

Though John Jeffries was the first person actually to go aloft on a scientific mission, he was not the first to use a balloon for research. That distinction belongs to the British manufacturer and engineer Matthew Boulton, a partner of James Watt, the inventor of the steam engine. On a dark summer night in 1784 Boulton sent up a small unmanned hydrogen balloon to which he had affixed a firecracker with a two-foot fuse. His purpose: to determine whether rolling thunderclaps are caused by a series of explosions or by the echoes of a single explosion. Boulton's fuse took so long to burn that his gas-filled balloon had drifted almost out of earshot from the launching site before the firecracker detonated and ignited the hydrogen. But those close enough to hear the explosion reported that it did indeed "growl like thunder."

Jeffries had more ambitious plans. His scientific goals, he wrote, were to determine the barometric pressure and temperature at various altitudes, and to observe air currents in order "to throw some new light on the theory of winds in general." As he was not himself a balloonist, Jeffries enlisted Blanchard's aid, and the two made their first free flight together from London on November 30, 1784. The flamboyant Blanchard carried along a quantity of self-promoting pamphlets to shower on the heads of those below. Jeffries took along vials for collecting air samples, a compass, a precision timepiece, an electrometer, a hygrometer, a thermometer and a barometer.

During their hour and a half aloft, Jeffries noted that the air temperature dropped considerably as the balloon rose, falling from 51° on the ground to 29° at 9,000 feet, the maximum altitude the balloon reached. He also recorded a steady decrease in barometric pressure during the ascent, and his hygrometer indicated an appreciable variation in the moisture content of the air at different altitudes. Jeffries concluded that little more could be learned on such a brief flight but hoped that longer scientific ascents would be forthcoming. Unfortunately for the cause of atmospheric research, when Jeffries joined Blanchard on their spectacular Channel crossing in January 1785, he was too busy trying to stay alive to collect much scientific data, and he never made another flight.

The next balloon to rise for science' sake was piloted by another Frenchman, Étienne Robertson, who cast off from Hamburg, Germany, on the morning of July 18, 1803. Robertson, more celebrated as an aeronaut than as a scientist, was accompanied on this five-and-a-half-hour flight by a friend named Lhoëst, a music teacher who lived in Hamburg. The two carried out a number of experiments. Robertson discovered that he could plunge his hand into boiling water without the slightest discomfort—the boiling point of water being considerably lower at high altitudes. But his report was rendered suspect by another claim that he made: The altitude, he said, caused his head to swell up so much that he could not put on his hat.

The following year a young French physicist, Joseph Louis Gay-

Lussac, made a carefully managed ascent from Paris that produced more credible results. Among other things, Gay-Lussac reported that his compass readings showed no apparent difference in magnetism at various altitudes up to 23,000 feet. He also collected a bottle of air at that altitude and found later that its components were the same as those in sea-level air. The 26-year-old scientist studied himself as well, discovering both his pulse and breathing rates to be "considerably increased" at an elevation of 4½ miles; his throat became so dry that it hurt to swallow. Evidently he experienced no swelling of his head.

Scientific ballooning came to a virtual halt after Gay-Lussac's ascent. In 1808 the Italian meteorologists Pascal Andreoli and Carlo Brioschi set a new altitude record by rising to 25,000 feet in a hot-air balloon. But with the exception of this and a few isolated and inconclusive experiments in Germany and England, aerial research yielded to an inertia that persisted until 1850, when it was revived by two French savants named Jean-Augustin Barral and Jacques Bixio.

Barral and Bixio intended to study such things as the composition of air and the changes in temperature and humidity at high altitudes. Unfortunately, they neglected an important first step: learning how to handle their balloon. Overinflated at launch, the hydrogen-filled bulb rose almost like a rocket to an altitude of nearly 20,000 feet. It was soon apparent that the netting around the balloon was too tight and the lines between the aerostat and the gondola were too short. As the gas in the balloon expanded with the increasing altitude, the fabric pushed downward, draping its bulk over the novice aeronauts. Trying desperately to seize the valve line and relieve the pressure on the dangerously bulging balloon, Barral and Bixio accidentally ripped a hole in the fabric, releasing a blast of gas that nearly asphyxiated them. The sudden loss of gas also precipitated a descent so rapid that the two men had to jettison their clothes and various other encumbrances—instruments excepted—to slow their fall. They negotiated a safe if inelegant landing.

Unintimidated by this experience, the two researchers reascended, more adroitly, a month later. This time they reached an elevation of 23,000 feet and became the first to learn that high-altitude cirrus clouds contained ice crystals. But their achievement was soon overshadowed by the accomplishments of two Englishmen whose feats would for a time make Great Britain the undisputed leader in high-altitude research.

Henry Coxwell and James Glaisher matched each other like a pair of mid-Victorian book ends. Both were fastidious, sober-minded, industrious and fearless men. Both possessed the kind of dignity and formality that makes it difficult to imagine them calling each other by their first names, even when alone in the sky. And both were well beyond the impetuosity of youth when they embarked on their tandem adventures for science in 1862—Coxwell was 43 and Glaisher 53.

Coxwell, the son of a naval officer, had abandoned a career as a dentist to become the successor to Charles Green as England's foremost balloonist. As a young man he had circumvented his parents' disapproval of his aerial avocation by ballooning at English pleasure gardens under the alias "Henry Wells." Glaisher, a distinguished meteorologist and a Fellow of the Royal Society, had developed an abiding curiosity about atmospheric phenomena during his youth while working as a surveyor in the mountains of Ireland. He was on the staff of the Greenwich Observatory in the late 1850s when he conceived the idea of a series of scientific balloon flights.

To Glaisher, the balloon had degenerated into a mere panderer to "air excursionists desirous of excitement" and feckless "seekers after adventure." But he believed that the sinner might still be saved and elevated to a nobler calling. Although his own experience with balloons was limited to gazing at them through a telescope, Glaisher won the support of the influential British Association for a program of flights that he hoped would peel away the manifold mysteries of the atmosphere.

A partial recounting of his scientific goals illustrates the scope of Glaisher's aspirations. His primary aim, he said, was to determine the temperature and moisture content of the air at different elevations. He also intended to examine the "electrical condition" of the air, to determine whether the "horizontal intensity" of the earth's magnetism was less or greater with elevation, and to collect air at different altitudes. Glaisher also planned to study the density and thickness of clouds, to determine the rate and direction of different wind currents in the atmosphere, to make observations on sound and on solar radiation and last, "to note atmospheric phenomena in general."

Glaisher's grand scheme clearly demanded both a balloon and a balloonist of excellence, and after a number of false starts he eagerly accepted when Coxwell offered to build a new aerostat with a capacity of 90,000 cubic feet especially for science. Glaisher rehearsed for his forthcoming adventures in his room, gathering his instruments around him in a compact area and taking a terrestrial observation or two for practice; this way, he explained later, "when the day for the ascent came, I was able to imagine that I was not making my aerial debut."

To minimize the danger of being blown out to sea, Coxwell chose as their launching site a spot in the English Midlands. Despite this sensible precaution, the first flight by the team of Coxwell and Glaisher, in July of 1862, had to be cut short abruptly when they drifted uncomfortably close to the North Sea at an altitude of some 23,000 feet. A second ascent in August was more felicitous: All the instruments functioned with gratifying precision as the balloon soared to 24,000 feet on a nearly windless afternoon. Coxwell, the accomplished aeronaut, was pleased to see that Glaisher was enjoying the ride; he had heard of some faint-hearted scientists who trembled so much while aloft that they were incapacitated. It was well that Glaisher took to the air so calmly, for his next flight with Coxwell, a few weeks later, would be one of the most harrowing sagas in the history of ballooning.

The two men lifted off at 1:03 p.m. on September 5, 1862, and climbed rapidly through a layer of clouds, emerging into radiant sunlight at an elevation of about 7,000 feet. At 1:22 they were 10,560 feet up and rising fast, reaching nearly 16,000 feet only six minutes later. At 21,000 feet the temperature had fallen to 8° F. and the oxygen content of the air was becoming thin. But still they shed ballast, ascending to a realm where no voyager had ever traveled before (and none has since without the aid of oxygen tanks or a pressurized cabin).

At 26,400 feet—fully five miles above the earth—with the temperature at two below zero, Glaisher's vision began to fade and he asked Coxwell to help him read his instruments. Then Glaisher saw that his companion had climbed onto the iron suspension hoop where the ropes of the rigging joined the ropes holding the gondola. Coxwell was trying desperately to unsnarl the valve line, which had become tangled as a result of the craft's recurrent rotation. If Coxwell could not reach the valve line and release some of the balloon's gas, the men would surely keep rising to almost certain doom.

Glaisher described the agonizing moments that followed: "I looked at the barometer," he wrote, "and found its reading to be 9¾ inches, still decreasing fast, implying a height exceeding 29,000 feet. Shortly after, I laid my arm upon the table, possessed of its full vigour, but on being desirous of using it I found it powerless." He tried to move the other arm, and found it powerless, too.

Glaisher shook himself, but his arms remained useless; when he tried to look at the barometer again, his head drooped to his left shoulder. "I struggled and shook my body again," he recalled, "but could not move my arms. Getting my head upright for an instant only, it fell on my right shoulder; then I fell backwards, my back resting against the side of the car and my head on its edge. I dimly saw Mr. Coxwell, and endeavoured to speak, but could not. In an instant, intense darkness overcame me."

While Glaisher was struggling in vain to remain conscious, Coxwell was fighting a losing battle in the rigging. His gloveless hands had become frostbitten, and he could not get a firm grip on the gyrating valve line. Finally he managed to free the twisted line so that it dangled to the gondola below. Then Coxwell eased himself down from his precarious perch and dropped to the side of his dazed companion. At this point, the two men were nearly 30,000 feet in the air, higher than anyone had ever ventured.

Still unable to grasp the vital valve line with his numbed fingers, Coxwell seized the line in his teeth. Jerking his head back and pulling with all his fading strength, he heard the lifesaving hiss of escaping gas—the valve had opened! The balloon began to descend at last into the oxygen-rich air below.

Coxwell then sought to rouse the prostrate Glaisher, who wrote later that he could hear his partner's voice but "could not see, speak or move." Coxwell persisted. "Do try; now do," he said, and Glaisher slowly began to stir. "The instruments became dimly visible," he recalled, "then Mr. Coxwell, and very shortly I saw clearly. Next I arose in

The climactic moment in the 1862 ascent of Englishmen James Glaisher and Henry Coxwell is set forth in this engraving. At 30,000 feet, Glaisher (right) sprawls unconscious in the thin air while Coxwell, his hands frozen by the cold, proceeds to save them by opening the balloon's gas-release valve with his teeth.

my seat and looked around as though waking from sleep, though not refreshed, and said to Mr. Coxwell, 'I have been insensible.' He said, 'You have, and I too, very nearly.' I then drew up my legs, which had been extended, and took a pencil in my hand to begin observations.''

As the balloon descended to the level of the clouds and passed through them, Glaisher returned to his methodical observations, and calculated that he had been unconscious for no more than seven minutes. "No inconvenience followed my insensibility," he concluded in his understated account of the adventure, "and when we dropped it was in a country where no conveyance of any kind could be obtained, so I had to walk between seven and eight miles."

The quiet valor of these two Victorians captured the imagination of their countrymen. Editorial writers and worshipful school children joined the scientific fraternity in hailing their feat. The London *Times* declared that scientific courage—"solitary, deliberate, calm and passive"—was more impressive than any other kind of heroism.

For Glaisher, however, the scientific yield of this and several later flights was more gratifying than national adulation. He had learned, among other things, that temperature does not uniformly decrease with altitude—the decline is rapid at lower elevations and then becomes more gradual. Humidity virtually disappeared, he reported, at altitudes above 25,000 feet. And contrary to Gay-Lussac's observations in 1804, Glaisher found that the strength of the earth's magnetism also declined with altitude. He also discovered a warm current of air blowing from the southwest; Glaisher correctly surmised that this phenomenon, combined with the Gulf Stream, caused the relatively mild English winters.

The bold venture of Glaisher and Coxwell into the upper air had set another balloon altitude record, but the fact that this distinction now belonged to Britain was viewed across the Channel in France as an affront to Gallic pride; the national rivalries that had waxed and waned through ballooning history now reappeared in the name of science. But the Frenchmen who contemplated bettering the mark of Coxwell and Glaisher realized that something more than will power was needed, and soon after the end of the Franco-Prussian War of 1870 and 1871 they produced that something: an oxygen-breathing apparatus that would permit aeronauts to operate without discomfort high above the earth.

The device consisted of a mouthpiece attached by a tube to a small balloon filled with a mixture of normal air and pure oxygen. It was first tested by scientists Joseph Crocé-Spinelli and Théodore Sivel in a vacuum chamber from which air could be pumped, thus simulating the lack of oxygen at increasingly high altitudes. The success of the preliminary tests encouraged them to recruit a balloonist for further experiments aloft, which might incidentally break the altitude record. Their choice was a gallant veteran of the balloon airlift during the Prussian siege of Paris, Gaston Tissandier.

Equipped with their oxygen containers, thermometers, barometers

Ballooning's peerless collector

Gaston Tissandier, the French scientist and patriot, had a valiant and varied career as an aeronaut: He carried mail and dispatches from Paris by balloon during the Prussian siege of 1870, and in 1875 he survived a high-altitude flight of the balloon *Le Zénith* on which his two scientist-passengers perished *(right)*. Later, while trying to develop a steerable balloon, he invented and success-fully tested an electric-powered dirigible.

But it was as a collector of balloon literature and memorabilia that Tissandier gained his greatest satisfaction. For 25 years, until his death in 1899, he filled his Paris home to overflowing with ballooning books, artwork and curios, amassing more than 3,000 objects in all—by his own reckoning "the most complete collection of its kind in the world."

Gaston Tissandier is surrounded by a portion of his beloved ballooning collection in the study of his Paris apartment.

Somber French villagers carry away the bodies of Théodore Sivel and Joseph Crocé-Spinelli, who were killed in 1875 by oxygen starvation during a high-altitude ascent in the balloon Le Zénith.

and an array of other instruments, the three men ascended from Paris in April of 1875 in the balloon *Le Zénith*. It was a beautiful spring day, and *Le Zénith's* open gondola rose in the warm sun toward a broad blue sky laced with cirrus clouds. At 14,000 feet the men tried the oxygen equipment. It was working perfectly.

The first signs of discomfort appeared at 23,000 feet. Sivel, feeling sick and drowsy, took a bracing pull of oxygen, and wrote in his log: "The effect is excellent." A few moments later Tissandier observed that the temperature was 10 below zero. "We are climbing," he scrawled in his notebook. "Crocé is panting. We are breathing oxygen. Sivel is closing his eyes. Crocé is also closing his eyes." They revived themselves and, determined to reach 30,000 feet, jettisoned more ballast and continued to rise.

Despite intermittent pulls on his oxygen tube, Tissandier could feel himself gradually weakening as they climbed past 25,000 feet. He felt lightheaded and strangely euphoric, but when he decided to take another gulp of oxygen he could not lift his arm. He tried to speak but the words would not come. Moments later he was unconscious.

When Tissandier revived, he discovered that *Le Zénith* was falling rapidly—driven down, he reported later, by strong winds. He had been unconscious for 38 minutes. Sivel and Crocé-Spinelli were lying on the

117

floor of the gondola with their eyes closed. Tissandier fainted again, only to be shaken awake by Crocé-Spinelli, who now made a grave mistake: Giddy from lack of oxygen but still eager to reascend, he threw out more ballast—along with an 80-pound piece of equipment and some blankets. Tissandier blacked out again as the balloon, suddenly lightened, shot upward to an altitude later estimated to be 28,000 feet.

When he regained consciousness more than an hour later, Tissandier saw that the balloon was descending once more with frightening speed. "I crept along on my knees and pulled Sivel and Crocé by the arm," he wrote later. " 'Sivel! Crocé!' I exclaimed. 'Wake up!' My two companions were huddled up motionless in the car, covered by their cloaks. I collected all my strength and endeavored to raise them up. Sivel's face was black, his eyes dull, and his mouth was open and full of blood. Crocé's eyes were half closed and his mouth was bloody."

Still shouting to his fallen comrades, Tissandier jettisoned the remaining ballast and eased Le Zénith to a bumpy but safe landing. Sivel and Crocé-Spinelli were dead, their bodies already cold and stiff.

Eulogized as ballooning's first martyrs to science, the two were laid to rest in Paris not far from the grave of Madeleine Blanchard, the first woman to be killed in a balloon. The most widely accepted explanation for their deaths was a shortage of oxygen—they had used their breathing devices only intermittently, instead of continuously as they should have. Why had Crocé-Spinelli and Sivel perished at high altitude while Tissandier—like Glaisher and Coxwell before him—survived? The answer was probably Tissandier's relatively better physical condition or his greater acclimatization to high altitudes. Glaisher had observed that the effects of altitude differed among individuals and even varied with the same person in different circumstances.

Whatever its causes, the tragedy was followed by a long hiatus in manned high-altitude research. Not until 1894 did a balloonist venture again into the far reaches of the atmosphere—and this time the experimenter was not French but German. Successfully using the same type of oxygen apparatus that had failed his French counterparts nearly two decades before, the meteorologist Arthur Berson piloted his hydrogen balloon to an elevation of 30,000 feet. In 1901, accompanied by Reinhard Süring, he established still another record, rising to 35,500 feet.

By this time manned scientific flights were again drifting out of favor. French researchers, perhaps chastened by the fate of Sivel and Crocé-Spinelli, pioneered the development of devices that could automatically record meteorological data and then be parachuted back to earth. The high-altitude balloonist, it seemed, had become excess baggage, and attention shifted to a new and perhaps even more forbidding frontier where balloons might help lead the way: the North Pole.

Polar exploration exerted the same hold on the late-19th Century imagination that space travel would in a later age. Expedition after expedition had boarded ships and sailed north into the frozen silence,

The dramatic filmed record of a doomed expedition

On August 6, 1930, two Norwegian walrus hunters put ashore from the sloop *Bratvaag* on desolate White Island, 900 miles north of the Arctic Circle. While searching for fresh water, they noticed the lid of an aluminum pot laid bare of ice by the mild summer. Half-buried a few yards away lay a human skeleton clothed in rotting arctic garb. In the coat's lining was sewed the monogram *A;* in its pocket was a diary. It contained the last written words of Salomon August Andrée, the celebrated Swedish aeronaut who, with colleagues Knut Fraenkel and Nils Strindberg, had vanished in 1897 while trying to fly to the North Pole. Thus was solved a mystery that had persisted since the trio's departure 33 years earlier from Dane Island, Spitsbergen *(below)*.

The remains of Fraenkel and Strindberg were found near Andrée's. So was most of the party's plentiful equipment, including—remarkably—several metal cylinders of exposed film, shot mainly by Strindberg. An expert photo-technician in Stockholm was assigned to try, as he said, "to waken to life the seed sown one third of a century ago." His efforts yielded some 20 reproducible photographs.

Several of these haunting images, damaged by years of exposure to arctic cold and moisture, are shown on the following pages.

KNUT FRAENKEL

SALOMON AUGUST ANDRÉE

NILS STRINDBERG

The Andrée expedition sets forth from Spitsbergen in the Ornen (Eagle) on July 11, 1897, bound for the North Pole, 700 miles away.

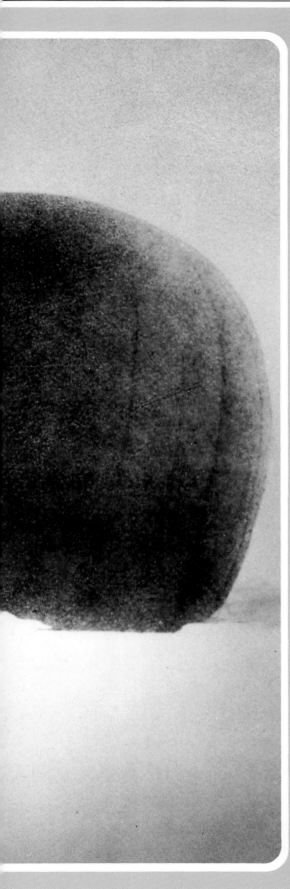

From atop the basket of the fallen balloon, Andrée (right) scans the horizon in search of land. According to his diary, all he saw was a lone bird and endless miles of ice.

In one of the recovered photographs, Andrée and Fraenkel examine their balloon, which had been forced down by a coating of ice three days after its takeoff.

After eight days, Andrée's party began walking toward an island 210 miles away where they had stored supplies. In this photograph, taken with the camera's automatic shutter, all three aeronauts push a sledge over a wall of pressure ice.

Fraenkel and Strindberg stand over a polar bear shot during their trek toward land. Bear meat became the aeronauts' main food, and it may have killed them: Bear remains found at the White Island campsite in 1930 were contaminated by trichinae, the parasites that cause trichinosis.

only to vanish for months or even years. When they finally straggled home, defeated, the explorers spoke of an impenetrable vastness of ice and shifting, unpredictable floes that made navigation impossible.

The idea that an airborne mission might succeed where seagoing attempts had failed had been suggested from time to time, but was routinely rejected. After all, no balloon had *ever* stayed in the air as long as a polar journey would require, much less in latitudes where a coating of ice on the balloon's surface could force an unplanned and potentially disastrous landing. There was also the problem of prevailing winds: A balloon expedition to the Pole would have to gamble on a southerly wind current to get it there and then carry it within range of the northernmost settlements. The obstacles appeared insurmountable to everyone except an earnest Swede named Salomon August Andrée.

Andrée had visited the United States during his youth and had formed a friendship with the American balloonist John Wise. Later he had joined an expedition studying polar phenomena at Spitsbergen, off the northern coast of Norway; still later he served as chief engineer in the Swedish patent office. Energetic, strong-willed and daring—"Be careful of health," he once admonished himself, "but not of life"— Andrée was equipped by both training and temperament for the venture he assigned himself.

In 1895, Andrée outlined his plan for a polar expedition, by balloon, in a series of well-received lectures in which he merged science with patriotism. The Swedes, he declared, had been "characterized for ages by the most dauntless courage," were familiar with the vagaries of the polar climate and "by nature herself trained to endure them." This appeal to national pride, coupled with Andrée's solid reputation, helped assure the expedition's financing: Sweden's King Oscar and the munitions maker-philanthropist Alfred Nobel were among the contributors.

The balloon that would convey Andrée and two carefully screened fellow voyagers on this singular expedition was custom designed. Andrée's meticulous specifications for the aerostat—which he named *Ornen (Eagle)*—called for a 170,000 cubic-foot envelope, made out of double Chinese silk to give it strength and durability. There was no valve at the top of the balloon, where it might be clogged by snow; instead, two valves were placed at different points in the lower section of the envelope. An extra layer of silk over the netting provided further protection against damage by snow or ice.

Andrée planned to control his altitude with three drag ropes, each 1,100 feet long and screwed together in sections, as well as several shorter lines. Three square sails were attached to horizontal poles above the car; it was hoped that they would permit a course variation of up to 30 degrees. The wicker gondola was enclosed, cylindrical and five feet deep; in it would be stowed three sleds, a canvas boat, three sleeping berths, a compact storehouse of tools, weapons, other supplies and enough food to last four months.

The departure was set for the summer of 1896 from a site on the northwestern tip of Spitsbergen, some 700 miles from the Pole. Andrée optimistically estimated that a steady southerly wind might propel the balloon over the Pole in three days; the landing site after that, depending on the wind direction, might be anywhere along the northern coasts of Siberia, Canada or Alaska. The *Ornen* was inflated with hydrogen and lodged in a "balloon house" 100 feet high to await the desired breeze, but the weather remained obstinate throughout July and well into August; by then the phantom arctic summer had already passed and it was too late to set out.

In 1897 the 43-year-old Andrée and his crewmen, Nils Strindberg and Knut Fraenkel, returned to Spitsbergen for another try. The high-spirited Strindberg, 24, was a physics instructor at Stockholm University and an accomplished amateur photographer. The 27-year-old Fraenkel was a muscular civil engineer with a fondness for mountain climbing. In preparation for the expedition, both men had learned ballooning in Paris. On July 11, after a six-week wait, the longed-for southerly wind finally stirred the water of the little harbor near their launching site. The moment had finally arrived, and the balloon was moved out of its shed. "Strindberg and Fraenkel!" shouted Andrée after everything had been checked one final time. "Are you ready to get in the car?" They were, and all three explorers scrambled into the gondola as the ground crew held the mooring ropes steady.

At 1:46 p.m., Andrée gave the order to cut the *Ornen* loose. The balloon rose sluggishly over the harbor and floated northeastward. Suddenly the craft dipped and touched the water, then rebounded and rose again as the explorers hurriedly dumped 455 pounds of ballast. The crewmen on shore watched excitedly until the balloon was a black dot on the northern horizon. Everything seemed to be going well, but Andrée knew that the expedition was already in trouble. The lower portions of the three long drag ropes—the most vital elements in Andrée's plan to control altitude and direction—had somehow come unscrewed during lift-off and were lying on the shore like great coiled snakes. The *Ornen* was now free-flying into the unknown.

The millions who had avidly followed the expedition's preliminary stages in newspapers around the world settled back to await word from the explorers. Whatever news was forthcoming would arrive via carrier pigeons or from buoys dropped from the balloon, the expedition's only means of communication. Four days after the *Ornen* took off, the captain of a Norwegian sealing vessel shot a pigeon perched in his ship's rigging. In a cylinder attached to the bird's leg was a message from Andrée, sent at midday on July 13 from a point about 200 miles north of their launch site. "Good speed to E. 10° S.," the message read. "All well on board. This is the third pigeon post." No other pigeons appeared, and the rest of the summer passed without further word. Then came autumn, and then the long night of the arctic winter. Still there was no news of Andrée and his crew. If they were still alive the explorers would be killing polar bears for food by now, and enduring the cold in whatever shelter they could improvise. Such makeshift survival was possible, to be sure—others had done it before. Strindberg's father remained optimistic: "One has to go on and hope for a year at least," he wrote, "and even after that don't draw too unfavorable conclusions."

A year passed, and more; search vessels went out, and returned without a clue. Then in February of 1899 came electrifying news: The bodies of the three Swedes had been found by primitive tribesmen in northern Siberia. The report proved to be false. Three months later, a message from Andrée was recovered from a buoy washed up on the coast of Iceland, but the communiqué had been dispatched less than 12 hours after the missing men's departure. A similar message turned up the following year on a Norwegian beach. By this time three years had gone by, and the presumption that the explorers were dead had hardened into certainty.

The fate of the *Ornen* remained unknown for 33 years. In the summer of 1930 a pair of walrus hunters off a Norwegian ship stumbled upon the skeletons of the three explorers in the bleak arctic fastness of White Island, about 280 miles from where the balloon had lifted off *(page 119)*. Astonishingly, the diaries, logbooks and letters that the men had written were still legible. This record told how the *Ornen,* accidentally freed of almost 1,200 pounds of drag rope, had climbed on the first afternoon to 2,270 feet, much higher than Andrée had intended. The wind drove the balloon steadily northeast on the first day, then west and then east again; during one 13-hour span it hung motionless when a dangling line snarled on a chunk of ice. Thick fog hampered visibility and a freezing drizzle coated the balloon with a heavy cargo of ice that lowered the craft until the cramped gondola smacked repeatedly against the ice—eight times in one 30-minute period.

Shaken but still in good spirits, the explorers treated themselves to an elaborate midday meal on July 13; that evening they jettisoned ballast and rose to an altitude where they could try their sails. Andrée described the effect as "quite stately," but the sails, as a century of predecessors could have told him, were utterly useless in controlling the balloon. Again forced downward by ice, the men spotted a huge polar bear only 100 feet beneath them. Early the next morning they were drifting slowly northeastward but flying so low that they were once more bouncing off pack ice; at 7:22 a.m. they touched down gently on an ice floe and stayed there. They had been in the air for 65 hours and had covered perhaps a third of the distance to the North Pole. They were 180 miles from the nearest land.

According to their diaries, the three men spent the next week loading their food and gear onto the sleds. They then began a desperate trek across the drifting ice in an effort to reach an emergency supply depot that they had established on Franz Josef Land, which was some 210 miles to the southeast. The terrain was so difficult that they could travel no more than three miles a day; on some days, forced backward by the constantly moving ice, they actually lost ground. When they came to the watery channels between floes, they piled the sleds on board the canvas boat and floated across.

In early August, realizing that they could not reach their goal before the onslaught of winter, they changed their course and headed for White Island, where they set up winter quarters in October. Precisely what happened then will never be known, though it appears that all three men died within weeks, possibly of food poisoning—defeated at last in their bid to complete the most ambitious scientific expedition that balloonists had ever attempted.

Andrée had no balloon-borne imitators, and by the time his remains were found men had reached the North Pole by both dog sled and airplane. But there was yet another frontier to be broached by balloon, a lofty, unexplored zone that stood at the threshold of outer space.

The stratosphere had not even been discovered when the Andrée party drifted north to disaster in 1897. The detection of this region between seven and 12 miles above the earth, a zone where the temperature does not decrease with altitude but remains constant, came as the result of unmanned balloon experiments conducted by a French meteorologist at the beginning of the 20th Century. By 1930, the year that the mystery of Andrée's disappearance was finally solved, balloonists had already launched an adventurous new era of stratospheric exploration.

The first of this new generation of scientific aeronauts was Captain Hawthorne C. Gray, a seasoned United States Army balloonist with more than 100 ascents to his credit. In 1927, Gray went aloft to study atmospheric conditions at altitudes above 40,000 feet and to determine the limits at which the human body could function. (It was widely believed at the time that the atmospheric pressure in the lungs would be too low at such heights to sustain life, even for a balloonist equipped with an oxygen mask.) He also hoped to break the German Arthur Berson's 35,500-foot altitude record, which had stood since 1901.

Gray made his first attempt on March 9, lifting off from a field near Belleville, Illinois. A combination of faulty oxygen equipment and over-exertion in emptying ballast bags caused him to pass out at 27,000 feet, and he returned to earth without rising higher. On May 4 he tried again, this time with an improved breathing system and ballast that could be dumped merely by pulling a cord. Wearing more than 60 pounds of flying clothes against the bitter cold, Gray listened to jazz beamed from a St. Louis radio station as his balloon rose through the clouds and toward a sky that he described as "deep, almost cobalt, blue."

By the time he reached 40,000 feet—well into the forbidding stratosphere—Gray had released all of his 4,700 pounds of sand ballast. Seeking to rise still higher, he secured a specially designed parachute to an emptied oxygen tank and heaved the tank over the side of his open basket. The steel cylinder weighed only 25 pounds, but the loss of its weight was enough to send Gray's balloon up to 42,470 feet, more than eight miles above the earth. No man had ever been so high before.

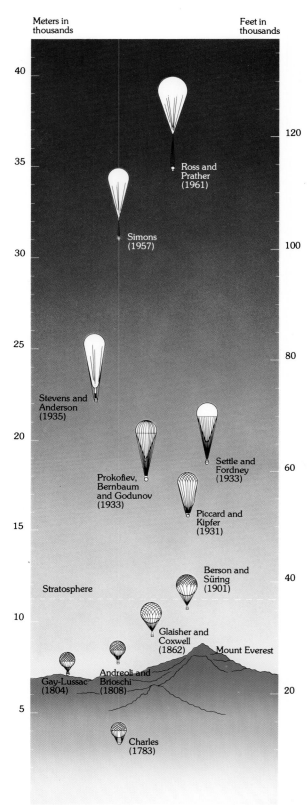

The ever-higher altitudes reached by two centuries of aeronauts are registered on the chart above by symbols resembling the original balloons in scale and shape.

Gray's descent was more dramatic. After tugging the valve line to release enough gas to start the balloon downward, he found himself plummeting earthward at a tremendous velocity as the gas contracted with increasing air pressure. Seeking to slow his fall, he began pitching more parachute-equipped oxygen tanks over the side. But the balloon continued to drop at a dangerous rate, and Gray soon saw that his likely landing spot was a swamp. At 8,000 feet, he scrambled to the rim of the basket, leaped into space and pulled the rip cord of his parachute, which brought him safely to earth.

Gray's parachute jump saved his life, but it also barred him from claiming an official altitude record—under rules laid down by the Fédération Aéronautique Internationale, the worldwide record-keeping organization, a balloonist had to stay with his craft from lift-off to landing in order to qualify for a record.

In November of 1927, Gray went aloft once more from Illinois. For the second time that year he reached 40,000 feet, but this time the cold air froze his clock and he was thus unable to determine whether he was using up his supply of oxygen. His handwriting became progressively weaker until he scratched out a final log entry: "sky ordinary deep blue—sun very bright—sand all gone." Soon afterward he lost consciousness and died, either from the exhaustion of his oxygen supply or from the shock that his lungs had suffered. The following day a farm boy discovered Gray's body, still in the gondola, in the branches of a tree near Sparta, Tennessee.

Gray's death convinced scientists that survival in the stratosphere demanded a sealed cabin that could maintain the atmospheric pressure that exists at ground level—the forerunner of the pressurized aircraft and space capsules of a later day. In 1930, the brilliant and innovative Swiss physicist Auguste Piccard, working in Brussels, devised such an enclosure, a spherical aluminum gondola that was also equipped with a system for reusing its own supply of air.

Piccard was a scholarly researcher who repeatedly professed his indifference to altitude records even as he was setting them. His real interest was in studying the origin and nature of cosmic rays, which he believed might someday be harnessed as a limitless source of energy. By May 27, 1931, the 47-year-old professor and his gondola were ready for their stratospheric debut.

Ascending before dawn from Augsburg, Germany, Piccard and a young assistant, Paul Kipfer, ran into serious trouble almost immediately. An instrument that was supposed to be inserted into a one-inch hole in the gondola's shell would not fit; the edge of the hole had been bent in a prelaunch mishap. Struggling to prevent the escape of their precious air through the hole, they finally plugged the opening with petroleum jelly and oakum. But their problems had only begun. The ingenious Piccard had painted one side of the ball-like gondola a heat-absorbing black and the other side a heat-reflecting white. He had provided a motor to rotate it so that the interior temperature would remain comfortable. Now he found that the motor had failed, with the black, heat-absorbing side turned toward the sun. The inside of the gondola became so hot that Piccard and Kipfer shed most of their clothes and quickly exhausted their small water supply.

Despite their discomfort, the two men rose steadily to a record altitude of 51,775 feet. There, as they were preparing to descend, they discovered that the valve line had twisted during takeoff and would not work. The only way they could get down was to wait for the relentless sun to set and for the 500,000 cubic feet of hydrogen in their balloon to cool and contract. Worried that they might run out of oxygen, they suffered through a seemingly endless descent before settling to earth at 9:30 p.m. on the slope of an Austrian glacier, barely missing the surrounding peaks and crevasses. They spent a chilly night on the glacier and scrambled down the mountain the next morning, meeting a rescue party on the way.

Piccard, citing the "mental distress" his adventure had caused his wife and four children, promptly announced that he intended to retire from stratospheric flight and return to more congenial pursuits in his laboratory. But his resolve soon eroded. On August 18, 1932, accompanied by a fellow physicist, Max Cosyns, he made a second ascent, this time from Zurich, Switzerland. Piccard had corrected the most serious oversight of his previous venture by designing a more effective way to control the valve line. But his attempt to solve the temperature problem by painting the gondola all white was less successful, and the cold was almost unendurable.

In every other respect the Zurich flight was an unalloyed triumph. Piccard broke his own altitude record, ascending to 53,152 feet while gathering important new information about the intensity and movements of the elusive cosmic rays. He had also become a celebrity—nearly 200 journalists were waiting for him when he emerged from his hotel on the day after his flight. From then on Piccard directed his energies to ocean diving, in a pressurized gondola he called a bathyscaphe, but in 1934 his twin brother, Jean, ascended in a balloon from Dearborn, Michigan, to study cosmic rays at 57,000 feet. Jean's pilot on this flight was his wife, Jeannette, who thus became the first woman in history to enter the stratosphere.

Auguste Piccard's triumphant demonstrations of his pressurized gondola were the technical preliminaries to an altitude race that soon began between two scientifically ambitious nations, the Soviet Union and the United States. The intent of the Russian ascents, which were sponsored by the government, and the American flights, conducted under the joint auspices of the National Geographic Society and the United States Army Air Corps, was unarguably scientific—instruments were carried aloft and data meticulously gathered. But the muscle flexing of rival technologies was equally obvious, for each of these stratospheric probes between 1933 and 1935 aimed higher than the one before. And

Swiss-born physicist and aeronaut Auguste Piccard (right) and his assistant, Paul Kipfer, model the upside-down wicker baskets stuffed with pillows they wore as shock-resistant headgear on their record ascent to 51,775 feet in May 1931.

the consequence was a predictable succession of conquests, near-misses and disasters.

The Russians were first to score when, in September of 1933, Georgi Prokofiev, Ernst Bernbaum and Konstantin Godunov made a record-breaking ascent to 58,700 feet. The 880,000-cubic-foot Soviet balloon—patriotically dubbed the *Stratostat U.S.S.R.*—was the largest yet constructed and was equipped with an electrical ballast-discharging system. Two months later the United States responded with a somewhat smaller craft, named *A Century of Progress* for the world's fair then going on in Chicago. Its crewmen, Navy Lieutenant Commander Thomas Settle and Marine Major Chester Fordney, rose from the municipal airport at Akron, Ohio, and ascended to 61,221 feet.

Not to be outdone, the Russians launched an even more elaborate balloon in January of 1934, but this time the result was catastrophic. While the craft was descending rapidly from a then-incredible altitude of more than 72,000 feet, the lightweight steel gondola suddenly broke free and plunged to earth, killing the three men.

The following July, a similar fate nearly overtook three American officers in the mammoth balloon *Explorer,* which was nearly three times

Almost a year after Piccard and Kipfer's flight, workmen on skis recover the heavy aluminum gondola from the Bavarian Alps. Until a museum in Brussels underwrote its recovery, the gondola—air travel's first pressurized cabin—had lain where it had landed, often defaced by passersby.

larger than the giant *Stratostat U.S.S.R.* Ascending before a Saturday afternoon crowd of some 30,000 spectators near Rapid City, South Dakota, the *Explorer* had reached 60,000 feet en route to a goal of 75,000 feet. Suddenly the crewmen—Major William Kepner, Captain Albert Stevens and Captain Orvil Anderson—heard a clattering on the roof of the gondola. Through their portholes they saw a huge rip in the lower section of the rubberized-cloth balloon. A direct hookup between the aeronauts and a radio network enabled millions of listeners on the ground to follow the drama that ensued. "There are now several tears in the underside," Kepner radioed as they started to descend. "I do not know what to expect."

The rip, later traced to a section of fabric that had weakened when two folds stuck together and then separated, worsened as the falling balloon gained momentum. At 20,000 feet the balloonists forced open the hatches and surveyed the damage. Not long afterward, the entire bottom section of the balloon fell away; the top half looked like an enormous parachute. "Bag badly torn up," they radioed urgently. "A good deal of surging of air. Descent very rapid."

At 6,000 feet, just as Kepner had ordered his two subordinates to prepare to bail out, the balloon suddenly exploded with a tremendous roar. Anderson leaped free almost immediately. Stevens tried twice to get through the hatch of the now-plummeting gondola but both times he was driven back by the rushing wind. Finally he managed to dive cleanly through the opening, and Kepner followed him a second later. As the three balloonists drifted slowly to the Nebraska cornfields below, their abandoned gondola hurtled past them and was smashed to bits when it hit the ground.

Kepner soon moved on to another assignment, but Stevens and Anderson went aloft again in November of 1935. To prevent another explosion, their balloon, *Explorer II,* was inflated with expensive but nonflammable helium instead of hydrogen. Rising once more from the South Dakota prairie, they peaked at a record altitude of 72,395 feet, and returned safely to earth with new information about cosmic rays, ozone and the ability of living spores to survive at high altitudes.

Explorer II would be the last of its generation of stratospheric balloons. The era of high-altitude excursions ushered in by Hawthorne Gray and Auguste Piccard ended as nations mobilized their resources for a second world war. But shortly after the War the idea of balloon-borne scientific missions was revived when the German-born American scientist Otto Winzen promoted the use of a strong and lightweight plastic material that would enable a balloon to carry heavier scientific payloads to altitudes approaching the edge of space.

Beginning in 1947, the United States Navy's Project *Skyhook* put Winzen's polyethylene balloons to work in a succession of unmanned flights. Laden with instruments that gathered data on cosmic rays and meteorological phenomena, the bubble-thin helium balloons were sent

A record leap from 20 miles up

Alone in the open gondola of his balloon, 102,800 feet above the New Mexico desert in 1960, Captain Joseph W. Kittinger Jr. of the United States Air Force uttered a simple prayer: "Lord, take care of me now." Then he jumped.

For the next four minutes and 38 seconds, the pressure-suited aeronaut fell at speeds up to 614 miles per hour, his descent slowed only slightly by an experimental six-foot-wide stabilization parachute that kept him from going into a violent—and probably fatal—spin. "I found myself on my back watching the balloon recede above me," he recalled. "Earth, sky and departing balloon revolved around me as if I were the center of the universe."

At 17,500 feet, Kittinger's main chute deployed automatically. Nine minutes later, having shattered world records for man's highest ascent and longest parachute drop, he lay on a bed of grass, sand and sage—uninjured, and grateful.

Captain Kittinger leaps from almost 20 miles up on August 16, 1960. The picture was taken by an automatic camera in the gondola.

131

aloft both from ground sites and from the decks of ships at sea; it was the *Skyhook* program that was later identified as the probable source of the flying-saucer reports.

By the mid-1950s the technology of high-altitude ballooning had progressed to the point where both the United States Navy and the Air Force were ready to resume the manned exploration of the stratosphere that had halted with *Explorer II* some 20 years before. By now, though, the goals of stratospheric flight were becoming more sophisticated. No longer limited to the collection of scientific data, the modern balloonists would be test pilots, measuring the capacities of both men and mechanisms to handle the unknown perils of space travel. The aeronauts would open the gates of space for the astronauts.

The first such test flight took place in the summer of 1956, when Navy Lieutenant Commanders Malcolm Ross and Morton Lewis, wired to instruments that automatically recorded their heartbeats and respiratory rates, launched the Navy's Project *Strato-lab* with an ascent in an open gondola to an altitude of 40,000 feet. Three months later the two men went up in a closed, pressurized gondola and reached 76,000 feet—surpassing the elevation attained by *Explorer II*—but a faulty valve forced them down before they could begin their high-altitude experiments. Captain Joseph W. Kittinger Jr. went even higher in June of 1957 on the maiden flight of the Air Force's Project *Manhigh,* rising to 96,000 feet in a cylindrical capsule only three feet in diameter. Kittinger, who had undergone 10 months of special training (including 24-hour claustrophobia tests) and who later in his career would make the longest parachute drop in history *(page 131),* wore a pressurized space suit so snug that he compared the sensation to "being loved by an octopus." His flight proved to be a heady experience. Responding to a radioed command that he begin his descent earlier than scheduled, the red-haired Kittinger was so exhilarated in his perch that he replied from 18 miles up: "Come and get me."

The second *Manhigh* flight, piloted by Air Force Major David G. Simons in August 1957, produced the best test yet of the challenges that waited in space. Simons, a physician who had grown up in Lancaster, Pennsylvania, the hometown of pioneer balloonist John Wise, reported both his physical and psychological reactions during a 32-hour ride that took him to a maximum elevation of 101,516 feet. Most interesting of all was a feeling that he called the "breakaway phenomenon," a sense of detachment so pronounced that it filled him with a reverie while simultaneously diminishing his capacity to think and react. A more immediate concern was the build-up of carbon dioxide in his capsule, which could be offset only by frequent gulps of oxygen.

Simons was high enough for long enough to enjoy man's first extended look at the blue-purple sky on the brink of space; he later described a color intensity "so low that it was hard to comprehend, like a musical note which is beautifully vibrant but so high that it lies almost beyond the ear's ability to hear." (Simons got his comeuppance when

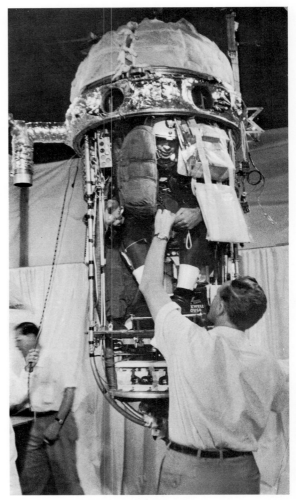

Packed into his cramped capsule, Major David G. Simons of the United States Air Force's Manhigh project adjusts his parachute with the help of flight director Otto Winzen. On his record 1957 ascent to 101,516 feet, Simons was in the three-by-eight-foot cabin for 43½ hours.

The United States Navy's Strato-lab IV begins its ascent to 81,000 feet in November 1959. The two aeronauts on board studied Venus through the 16-inch reflecting telescope atop their gondola and brought back data indicating the presence of water vapor, potentially capable of supporting life, in Venus' atmosphere.

he returned to earth. He had risen higher than any aeronaut in history, but a boy who ran up to him shortly after he landed on a South Dakota field turned away from Simons' balloon to gaze in wonder at the helicopter arriving to pick him up. "Look!" the boy cried, "I've always wanted to see one of them.")

As both Russia and the United States edged closer to manned space flight, it grew increasingly clear that the days of manned high-altitude balloon flights were numbered. The last major American effort was a voyage to 113,740 feet in May of 1961 by two United States Navy *Strato-lab* aeronauts, Malcolm Ross, now a full commander, and Lieutenant Commander Victor Prather. It was appropriate, perhaps, that their flight, which was designed to test the space suits developed for the Mercury astronauts, proved to be an even greater test of classic ballooning skill. Stymied by their failure to descend from peak altitude in spite of repeated valving, Ross and Prather released too much helium and finally started falling so fast that they had to throw out much of their equipment to avoid cracking up as they landed in the Gulf of Mexico. Then, in a tragic climax reminiscent of the fates of earlier aeronauts, the 34-year-old Prather fell into the water and drowned while attempting to scramble onto a hook dangling from a rescue helicopter.

A season in society

By the early 1900s ballooning was no longer the exclusive province of scientists, showmen and the military. Well-to-do sportsmen and -women on both sides of the Atlantic had embraced it as an entertaining diversion; weekend jaunts and races—won by the balloon that traveled farthest or that landed closest to an appointed spot—became the fashionable pastime at resorts and suburban parks.

Ballooning for sport got its start in France, where the wonders of lighter-than-air flight had first been demonstrated in the late 18th Century. But society balloonists probably enjoyed their finest hour in Edwardian England. There, from the well-tended grounds of exclusive polo clubs such as Ranelagh and Hurlingham, both near London, elegant aeronauts enlivened the summer season with free-flight competitions and pleasure voyages, frequently provisioned with fine food and chilled champagne.

Bearing well-dressed merrymakers serenely through the air, the early sport balloons were symbolic of that gilded, carefree era before Europe's old order was shattered by a devastating world war. Yet their popularity presaged a later day when ballooning for fun would become a pastime for thousands of people of every social class.

Smartly uniformed young men in white ducks, dark blazers and straw hats maneuver a balloon into position on a polo field at Ranelagh for a 1907 race sponsored by a member of Britain's elite Aero Club.

Rising above an audience of ladies in elaborate bonnets and gentlemen in morning dress, a flag-trimmed racing balloon sets out from Hurlingham, near London, on a spring day in 1908.

5

The challenge and joy of a precarious sport

Frank Hedges Butler was bored. The automobile that was to have taken him on a motor tour of Scotland had been wrecked and he was stranded in London during the summer of 1901. But Hedges, an Edwardian gentleman of independent means who had filled much of his life with travel to the far corners of the world, was determined not to be deprived of an adventure of some kind. So he turned to the latest diversion of the sporting set among Europe's upper classes and hired a balloon.

With his daughter, Vera, and his friend Charles S. Rolls, who would become well known as a manufacturer of superb motorcars, Butler went aloft for two hours over London. The flight made addicts of them all. So thrilled were they that, before coming down, they decided to establish a ballooning club. As Butler wrote later, "the resolution subscribed to in the air was soon put into terrestrial practice"; before the year was out the Aero Club of the United Kingdom had been founded as a branch of the national Automobile Club, itself only four years old.

Britain's Aero Club was not the first; France, Belgium and Austria already had active organizations and several other countries would soon follow suit. Balloons, if no longer the sensational crowd thrillers they once had been, were being adopted as playthings by the monied aristocrats. Soaring across a bucolic landscape not yet sullied by power lines or obscured by smog, the blue-blooded aeronauts of this gilded age could fully appreciate the leisurely grace of powerless flight. As one of them put it rather huffily after the first airplanes emerged, balloons were still "the only gentleman's way of going into the air."

Ballooning soon acquired a style to match the means and the tastes of its practitioners. Abercrombie & Fitch, the New York emporium for well-heeled adventurers, offered for sale an imaginative selection of ballooning accessories: rucksacks, flasks, sandbags, sand scoops for metering ballast, megaphones for communicating with the ground and with other balloons, and even a portable washbasin for those determined to emerge spotless from their aerial ventures. For those who wished merely to test the air, Abercrombie's would arrange an ascent with an experienced aeronaut. A short flight might cost $200 for the balloon, plus gas at one dollar per 1,000 cubic feet to fill it.

Exclusive clubs like the one Frank Hedges Butler was instrumental in founding hired the last of ballooning's showmen as instructors and mechanics. If a member fancied a moonlit cruise with his dinner guests,

In the basket of their balloon, the Elfe, the Italian team of Ettore Cianetti (left) and Alfred Vonwiller are the first to lift off in the staggered start of the Gordon Bennett race in 1906. It was the inaugural of an international contest that was to dominate sport ballooning until World War II.

he had only to ring up the mechanic and ask him to inflate one of the club's balloons, usually with coal gas, then proceed to the gasworks with his friends, who might still be dressed in formal attire.

Such a flight could indeed be a refreshing experience. Ascending at about 9 p.m. one evening in early May of 1906, Butler, by now a qualified aeronaut with 59 ascents recorded in his logbook, set out from London with two friends, their destination Brighton on the Channel coast. "The first thing that struck us," wrote Butler, "was the marvellous effect of the lights of London. Imagine millions on millions of lights, like a vast starry firmament, only upon the earth itself."

Shifting winds kept changing the balloon's course and made it necessary for Butler's party to descend from time to time to determine their location or to "rest," as he expressed it—no inconvenience since they preferred to reach Brighton with the light of dawn. At one of these stops, he recounted, "we dropped, thoroughly mystified as to our whereabouts, in a rookery" atop a large tree. The incursion aroused the birds living there into raucous complaint, which awakened the master of a nearby house. There then occurred, said Butler, the following unlikely discussion.

"Goodness gracious!" exclaimed the man, raising the window. "Who are you?"

"Balloonists, resting," replied Butler. "Where are we?"

"Twelve miles from Brighton going south. Are you stuck?"

"Oh, no, we're very happy. You don't mind us sitting on top of your tree, do you?"

"Not at all," said the man, who then closed the window with a polite "Good night."

Some two hours later, Butler and friends alighted near Brighton, and by 10 a.m. they had returned overland to London.

Butler's daughter, Vera, did not make that trip, but ever since her first ascent she had been an enthusiastic advocate of ballooning—for women as well as men. In a published article entitled "Ballooning for Ladies," she warned realistically that there was "all the difference between a 'hard' and a 'soft' descent." She described one rough landing on which the basket overturned and she and her two companions "were ignominiously decanted in a tangle of arms, legs, ropes, and sundries."

Vera Butler fretted that her post-Victorian friends might think her excessively adventurous. But women, she contended, were particularly susceptible to the enchantment of ballooning because "their imagination is said to be keener and more receptive than that of men."

The Contessa Grace di Campello della Spina, an Italian aficionada who flew over the Apennine Mountains on her honeymoon, was an impressionable balloonist of the kind that Vera Butler had in mind. "Sport of the gods!" exclaimed the Contessa after her crossing. "Who else flies over a sleeping world, through space, and knows the joy of motion without movement, without sound, without effort?" The Contessa thoughtfully appended a list of essential baggage for female aeronauts. It included "a small *nécessaire*"—a receptacle for relieving oneself—"a 'first aid,' a change of underwear, a light volume by a favorite author, a map and a guidebook."

If many society balloonists were content to reflect on the gentler aspects of their sport, aeronauts of greater mettle thirsted for the challenge of competition. They arranged races against those of similar bent, or challenged the record book in efforts to extend the limits of distance and endurance. They used balloons to overcome natural barriers—deserts, mountain ranges and expanses of open water. For these sportsmen, success was paramount—and synonymous with pleasure. They stood ready to jeopardize their balloons and even their lives as they pitted wit, skill and luck against one another and against a more formidable foe, the weather, in contests that soon achieved Olympian stature.

One of the first of the gentlemen-competitors was Count Henri de La Vaulx. In a race sponsored by the Aero Club of France in 1900, Count de La Vaulx stayed aloft for nearly 36 hours, coasting eastward through the bracing October atmosphere at altitudes that ranged as high as 18,810 feet. Before coming down he traveled 1,195 miles, from Paris well into Russia, not only winning the race but establishing distance and endurance records that stood for a dozen years. De La Vaulx enjoyed guessing what country he happened to be crossing and speculating on what kind of reception he might be accorded by the people below, should he land there. "Ah, there is nothing like the zest that comes of this uncertainty," he declared.

A flight across Europe could be zestful indeed: Conscientious border guards sometimes opened fire on trespassing aerostats, and de La Vaulx himself spent the first 24 hours after his record-setting flight to Russia in one of the Czar's jails. On his return home, he was asked whether his captivity had been a great hardship. "Yes," the Count replied with the sang-froid of his caste and calling, "the Russian officers persecuted me by the opening of so many bottles of French champagne that I was in great distress."

The national ballooning clubs of several nations were soon sponsoring races like the one that took de La Vaulx to Russia. Competition between nations, however, occurred only sporadically and informally until 1906, when the French formed the Fédération Aéronautique Internationale (F.A.I.) to establish standards and maintain records for the burgeoning world of aviation, which by then included the airplane. In that same year, flight in all its forms acquired a generous and enthusiastic patron—publisher-sportsman James Gordon Bennett of *The New York Herald.* Bennett, a flamboyant personality who spent most of his time in Paris, had already created, in 1902, a trophy for automobile racing and, hoping to stimulate progress, decided to do the same for aviation. He wanted the races to be open to any kind of aerial conveyance, but the F.A.I. decided to limit entries to lighter-than-air craft and later excluded even dirigibles (steerable, motorized balloons), which,

like airplanes, were still in their infancy in 1906. These far-sighted rulings prevented powered aircraft from eventually usurping the balloon races and prompted Bennett in 1909 to establish yet another racing trophy specifically for airplanes.

The first Gordon Bennett International Balloon Race started from Paris in late September of 1906. Altogether seven countries were represented by 16 balloons. Almost all of the pilots were virtuosos, survivors of national elimination races held earlier in the year in their respective countries. Count de La Vaulx and one of his stiffest competitors, Jacques Balsan, were to represent France, each in his own balloon; Britain sent two balloons manned by the cofounders of its Aero Club, Charles S. Rolls and Frank Butler.

The United States also fielded two entrants. The more famous of these—and probably the most recognizable of all the contestants— was the mustachioed and diminutive Alberto Santos-Dumont, a Brazilian who had spent most of the past decade experimenting with dirigibles in France. Santos-Dumont was flying under United States auspices

The Honorable Charles S. Rolls, motorcar magnate and a cofounder of the Aero Club of the United Kingdom, ascends in his balloon, the Imp, at a 1909 air regatta. On non-solo flights, the sometimes impish Rolls was known to entertain passengers by playing tunes on a child's toy whistle.

because Brazil was not a member of the F.A.I. His balloon, named *Les Deux-Amériques (Two Americas),* was equipped with a small engine and propellers to push it up or down so that it could fly without ballast.

The other American contender was United States Army Lieutenant Frank P. Lahm, who was in France attending cavalry school. Lahm was a late-hour substitute for his father, a more experienced balloonist, whose plans to compete in the race were sidetracked by his daughter's wedding back home. Because the senior Lahm had departed France without ordering a new balloon, Frank had to content himself with an old, patched-up one he purchased from Count de La Vaulx.

Besides the pilot, each balloon carried an assistant and provisions for three days. Lahm chose fellow officer Major Henry B. Hersey, who had recently returned from a daring but unsuccessful attempt to reach the North Pole by airship. Starting times were determined by lottery, and Lahm and Hersey, drawing No. 12, took off from the Tuileries gardens at 4:55 p.m. before a crowd estimated at 200,000.

From start to finish, the race proceeded almost as if it had been choreographed. Initially the wind carried the balloons southwest toward the Atlantic, an inauspicious beginning that could have dulled the competition by forcing all of them to land prematurely to avoid drifting over open sea. At a propitious moment the wind changed, wafting the racers north toward the English Channel and southern England.

Frank Butler, along with more than half the contestants, elected to set down in France rather than cross the Channel at night. But others, among them Lahm, Count de La Vaulx, Jacques Balsan, Charles Rolls and Alfred Vonwiller, in the single Italian balloon, accepted the challenge. They all made it successfully, and the fog of early morning found them coasting northward over England. Because Lahm's course had taken him farther inland than the others *(map, page 147),* he could travel farther north before reaching a new hazard, the North Sea. In midafternoon he landed at last in a Yorkshire pasture owned by a country squire who, upon signing Lahm's landing certificate as required by the rules of the race, declared that "an earthquake could not have caused more excitement" than the landing of the Americans' balloon. Lahm had traveled 402 miles in 22 hours 15 minutes, beating the Italian balloon by 31 miles to win the race. He shared the 12,500-franc prize with Major Hersey and returned home in triumph, bearing to the United States its first international trophy in aerial competition and the honor of hosting the next year's race. Only one incident had marred the event. Santos-Dumont, soon after takeoff, caught his sleeve in his balloon's propeller, which wrenched his arm painfully and forced him to retire.

With the Gordon Bennett Cup as their own annual Olympics, sport balloonists now attained a stature that their circus-aeronaut predecessors of the 19th Century had never quite achieved. Sanctioned by the F.A.I. and eagerly contested by the best balloonists from an expanding roster of nations, the Cup races helped ballooning retain its appeal at a time when faster, if noisier, forms of air travel were swiftly overtaking it.

Through the pre-World War I years the site of the race hopscotched from Paris to St. Louis to Berlin to Zurich, back to the United States and then to Germany and France again. Inevitably, sport ballooning was caught up in the nationalistic fervor that intensified as war approached. The fact that French balloonists held most of the records inspired a German, Hugo Kauleu, to establish a new benchmark of 1,756 miles on a 1913 solo flight to Siberia. In February 1914 a German crew outdid their own countryman with a flight of 1,897 miles—a record that would endure for 62 years. So far into the Siberian wasteland did these Germans go that, once landed, they had to mush by dog sled through shoulder-deep snow to the closest village. Then they languished three months in jail while diplomats negotiated their release.

Such boundary-crossing ventures, along with the Gordon Bennett Cup race itself, were suspended at the outbreak of war in August 1914. In 1920 the race was resumed with vigor, and three years later the contest occasioned the most catastrophic day in ballooning history.

Seventeen balloons from six nations had entered the 1923 race, which was to begin on the afternoon of September 23 from a plain outside Brussels. Weather was a problem from the start. Torrential rain pelted the aeronauts as they struggled to inflate their balloons. Violent gusts of wind battered the bulging globes and set them dancing wildly on their mooring ropes; one of the three American entries, the *St. Louis*, burst from the strain. Belgian officials consulted their rule books and reported that there was no provision for postponement due to foul weather; the race must go on. One by one the aeronauts lurched into the darkening sky and were borne northward before the storm.

The bad weather grew worse. As an American balloon piloted by Army officers Robert Olmstead and John Shoptaw took off, it collided with a still-unlaunched Belgian balloon. The Americans' gondola ripped the net containing the envelope of the Belgian entry, forcing it to withdraw. The American craft, apparently undamaged, climbed uncertainly into low clouds sporadically illuminated by streaks of lightning.

The only way to escape the storm was to climb above it, but even that tactic was no guarantee of safety. French crewmen aboard the balloon *Savoie* dumped 600 pounds of ballast and ascended so high that they encountered a blizzard. The snow coated their envelope and forced them down so precipitously that the men had to climb into the rigging to avoid injury when their basket slammed into the ground.

At lower altitudes the conditions were terrifying. The Swiss balloon *Genève* was struck by lightning at about 1,000 feet; it caught fire and fell to earth, killing its two crewmen instantly. *Polar,* entered by Spain and flown by Penaranda Baroa and Gomez Guillamon, had just climbed to 3,500 feet when it too was hit by a lightning bolt that killed Baroa outright and ignited the lower part of the envelope. The top half formed a parachute that braked the balloon's plunge; Guillamon leaped to avoid the flames when he was 100 feet above the ground. Landing in a soft, brush-filled swamp, he survived with two broken legs.

The James Gordon Bennett trophy above, which was presented to the 1929 winners of ballooning's most important race, was the third one created for the contest. Two of its predecessors had been retired, by Belgium in 1924 and by the United States in 1928, after balloons from those nations had won the competition three years in a row.

Publisher James Gordon Bennett's bulldog expression in this 1916 photograph befits his reputation as a tenacious, as well as generous, patron of early-20th Century sport. In addition to endowing the annual balloon race that bore his name, Bennett established similar prizes for airplane, automobile and yacht racing.

The next victims of the lightning were Olmstead and Shoptaw, the Americans who on takeoff had collided with the Belgian balloon. About three hours into their flight, as they crossed the frontier into the Netherlands, their balloon was struck and set afire. The flame-licked basket banged to earth near the town of Nistelrode, killing the two aeronauts.

A final accounting of this disastrous contest showed that six balloons had been destroyed, including the two wrecked on the ground. Of the 34 balloonists, five had died, five others were injured and two more had to be rescued from the sea off Denmark.

Responding to suggestions that the event be abandoned or at least held at a time when storms were less likely, the president of the Belgian Aero Club replied steadfastly that the balloonists preferred early-autumn races in Europe because strong westerly winds were normal for that season. Calmer conditions, he said, would make for a less interesting race. Callous as his words sounded, the Belgian was in fact expressing an attitude that most balloonists shared: Their sport was risky by definition, and uncertain weather added spice to the adventure. The Gordon Bennett race continued to be held annually—and usually in the autumn—for another 15 years, except for the Depression year 1931, when it was suspended because only one European entrant could raise the funds to travel to the United States, the host country.

That balloonists could finance their favorite competition in all but one year of the Depression would seem proof that the sport was still popular. In fact, however, the money came from a few select sources in each nation: wealthy patrons, large companies and the armed forces. Unhappily, balloons seemed to be losing their capacity to attract attention, chiefly because of competition from faster aircraft. Dirigibles and airplanes, advancing in dramatic technological leaps after World War I, had become more newsworthy than the graceful but old-fashioned aerostats. A single issue of *The New York Times* in 1928 provided an example: News of that year's national balloon race in Pittsburgh, in which three aeronauts died in a violent storm, was overshadowed by stories about two German aviators blazing a new transatlantic route via the Arctic Circle, about a Californian bent on setting an endurance record for a monoplane, about an Italian dirigible missing in the Arctic, and about two Spanish aviators overdue en route from Seville to Pakistan. Thus the news, 11 years later, that the 1939 Gordon Bennett Cup race had been canceled—Poland, the host country, having been invaded by Germany—rated little more than a footnote in the rush of events.

The apathy that had settled over sport ballooning showed signs of becoming a permanent affliction after World War II. Of the best lighter-than-air gases, hydrogen was considered too explosive, helium was too expensive and that venerable stand-by, coal gas, was in short supply. Moreover, the uncrowded vistas that had beckoned the aeronauts of another day were becoming filled with obstacles dangerous to vehicles so obstinately unmaneuverable as balloons. Power lines could slash their rigging and ignite their envelopes. The expanding volume of airplane traffic over every major city and in the air routes between them raised the specter of collision on every ascent. Relegated to isolated appearances at fairs and carnivals, balloons seemed to have become anachronisms in an age that could spare no time for their foolish antics. Though they did not quite become extinct, in either Europe or America, a 1959 United States census turned up only 14 airworthy balloons.

To write off balloons, however, was to ignore the uncanny resilience they had demonstrated during their nearly 200-year history. And, sure enough, by the 1960s their popularity was on the rebound again, thanks in large measure to the United States Navy. Searching for ways to send unmanned research balloons aloft for longer flights at low cost, the Navy in 1956 had pioneered new investigations into the oldest kind of aerostat—a hot-air balloon no different in principle from the montgolfiers that had enchanted Europe in the 1700s. Instead of paper or cotton for the envelope, the Navy used ultralight nylon or polyester. Instead of a straw fire, a propane burner heated the air inside.

The Navy's burner roared like a dragon once lighted, and flamed until its fuel was exhausted. The key next step, to extend the burner's endurance, was the accomplishment of a taciturn American balloonist named Ed Yost. Yost had designed and flown gas balloons while serving in the Navy and had helped the Navy design its hot-air balloons after he became a civilian. In 1960 he added a manually controlled valve to the burner, allowing the flame to be turned on and off as needed. He hung a basket from a hot-air balloon thus equipped and staged a public demonstration in a 95-minute flight across the South Dakota prairie.

With Yost's burner, aeronauts could inflate their balloons quickly and, as long as the fuel supply lasted, could rise or fall at will. Equally important, the abundance and relatively low cost of propane (at the time, $20 would buy about enough for a one-hour flight) served to democratize ballooning; the sport was now within the economic reach of any middle-class adventurer who could afford, say, a second car.

Dormant ballooning clubs soon revived and new organizations blossomed to satisfy the yen for camaraderie felt by a growing roster of aeronauts. The Balloon Federation of America was formed in 1961 and in 1964 the British Balloon and Airship Club was founded. (Ever mindful of tradition, the Britons assembled in the same rooms where Frank Butler and fellow members of the Royal Aero Club had once traded improbable stories.) After a relatively slow start, membership in the Balloon Federation of America, accounting for about 80 per cent of the balloonists in the United States, exploded in number from 66 in 1970 to 517 in 1974 and to 1,711 in 1979. The rolls in France, West Germany and several other nations multiplied proportionately.

It was not long before the urge to compete, which had disappeared with the demise of the Gordon Bennett Cup races at the start of World War II, came to life again. Hot-air balloons do not readily lend themselves to distance races—it is impractical for them to carry more than

Racing at the whim of the winds

The enduring appeal of the Gordon Bennett Cup balloon race lay in its suspense. No one, including the competitors, knew beforehand where or when the race would end. Once the balloons took off, they became captives of the wind; the winner was the one that traveled farthest before touching down.

For the inaugural race from Paris on September 30, 1906, there were sixteen balloons from seven countries that answered—at five-minute intervals—the starting gun fired by newspaper publisher Bennett himself. At first, as shown on the contemporary map at right, the contestants glided westward across France, then northward in the direction of the English Channel. Seven crews braved the crossing and reached England. Of these, the balloon *United States,* flown by Army Lieutenant Frank P. Lahm and Major Henry B. Hersey, continued along the westernmost course and thus could travel farther over land before approaching the North Sea. After 402 miles and more than 22 hours in the air, the *United States* touched down north of Hull to become the winner.

The paths and touch-down points of the 16 contestants in the first Gordon Bennett Balloon Race are plotted on this panoramic map of northern France and southern England, published two weeks after the race in the magazine La Vie au Grand Air.

two or three hours' fuel—so modern balloonists began to compete in other events, such as hare and hounds, a venerable contest of British ancestry in which chase balloons try to land as close as possible to a pace-setting balloon. They also engaged in the tumbleweed drop, an American creation that rewards the balloon-borne bombardier who can drop closest to a target a clump of tumbleweed, the desert plant noted for its erratic meanderings on the wind.

Contemporary balloonists congregate at festivals, such as the U.S. National Hot-Air Balloon Championships held annually in Indianola, Iowa, and the Albuquerque International Hot-Air Balloon Fiesta *(pages 162-169)*. Albuquerque, which entered the 1970s barren of balloons, soon evolved into the self-styled ballooning capital of the world, a claim supported by its resident population of more than 100 aeronauts. And in 1979 the Gordon Bennett Cup itself was revived, after a 40-year pause, in a race for gas balloons in Long Beach, California.

Just as hot-air balloons, because of their fuel limits, are unsuited to distance races, they are inadequate for another category of adventure that has challenged aeronauts ever since 1785, when Jean Pierre Blan-

Wearing civilian clothes for the occasion, Lieutenant Frank P. Lahm (left) and Major Henry B. Hersey stand proudly in the basket of their balloon, which they had named the United States, at the start of the inaugural Gordon Bennett race.

chard and Dr. John Jeffries first crossed the English Channel—namely, the conquest of the world's natural barriers by balloon. More than any other ballooning test, an assault on a mountain range or an ocean represents the peak of daring, the epitome of personal risk. For the goal is named in advance, and an untimely landing can easily be fatal.

Over the years, crossing the Channel by gas balloon had become almost commonplace. Other barriers fell too, though not *every* attempt at them was successful. In 1812, Britain's James Sadler tried and failed to cross the Irish Sea; five years later his son Windham succeeded. Francisque Arban, flying from Switzerland to Italy in 1849, became the first aeronaut to cross the Alps, but in 1901 contrary winds thwarted France's premier gentleman-balloonist, Count de La Vaulx, in his effort to cross the Mediterranean to Africa. He managed to land on the deck of a Navy cruiser fortuitously positioned in his path.

Well into the 20th Century, the only balloonists to have crossed the Atlantic were fictional, the heroes of a convincing but fraudulent account of a voyage from Wales to South Carolina, written in 1844 by Edgar Allan Poe and published as fact in the *New York Sun.* In 1873, daredevil American balloonist Washington Donaldson and two journalists had become the first men actually to try the Atlantic; they got no closer than Long Island Sound before a storm forced them down.

The dream of conquering the ocean persisted in the minds of modern balloonists, who had tools for the task that were unknown to their 19th Century forebears—lightweight plastic envelopes, radios, sophisticated weather-forecasting methods and, if they wished to use them, enclosed protective capsules of the kind Auguste Piccard had developed for high-altitude flights in the 1930s. But if technology had brought a transatlantic voyage temptingly within reach, the flight itself remained a supreme test of skill and a long-odds gamble with nature.

Arnold Eiloart and Colin Mudie were veteran English yachtsmen who had sailed across the Atlantic, but had never even ridden in a balloon. Nevertheless, one winter evening in 1957 they began planning to tackle the ocean by air. Soliciting advice from more experienced hands, they quickly qualified as balloon pilots and designed the *Small World,* a 53,000-cubic-foot hydrogen aerostat with a seaworthy gondola that could be converted to a sailboat if circumstances required.

After recruiting Mudie's wife, Rosemary, as photographer and Eiloart's 21-year-old son, Tim, as radio operator, the two yachtsmen lifted off in December from the Canary Islands, 180 miles off the African coast. They reckoned that the reliable northeast trade winds in those latitudes would carry them the 2,700 miles to the West Indies in about eight days. And so they might have done, had not the *Small World* run into a succession of vigorous updrafts that repeatedly forced the aeronauts to valve precious hydrogen to slow their ascent and remain at a safe altitude. No sooner had this emergency passed than the balloon became too heavy, falling so fast and so often that they eventually had to jettison their radio and some of their food to stay airborne. The flight,

An epidemic of spills, collisions and crash landings

The surge of interest in sport ballooning in the first decade of the 20th Century was accompanied by an alarming increase in the number of balloon-related accidents, injuries and deaths. And, because such mishaps were out of the ordinary and often spectacular, they received full play in the popular press.

Reporters and photographers were seldom present to record the incidents firsthand. But that was of little concern: Artists and journalists of the day could be counted on to produce a graphic and grisly—if sometimes overdramatized—re-creation worthy of the front page.

"Up to the present time," reported the magazine *Le Petit Parisien* with some relish on July 8, 1906, "when one has heard reports of collisions on the railroads, it has only been a question of accidents—more or less deadly—between trains, or of crashes with cars, wagons or herds of animals. This time, it is a balloon." The illustration that accompanied the article *(below, right)* details the misfortune of an aeronaut whose low-flying hot-air balloon crossed the tracks near Herbesthal, Germany, at precisely the wrong moment. "Fortunately it was a glancing blow," said the magazine; the balloonist escaped uninjured.

Far less fortunate was the misadventure of three Frenchmen who went up for a pleasant day in the air in May of 1904. Their coal-gas balloon, *Le Touriste*, was caught in a sudden spring squall, forcing them to make an emergency landing in a crowded residential district of Paris. Despite the balloonists' pleas to those in the neighborhood to stop smoking and to shut their windows, gas from the balloon was ignited by embers from a fireplace, and exploded. The ensuing fire damaged several homes and caused at least one death, making sensational copy for *Le Petit Parisien*. Its lurid account was embellished by the illustration at left, below.

Parisians scramble for cover as the balloon Le Touriste explodes in flames.

About to collide with a locomotive, an imperiled aeronaut holds on for his life.

Two Americans in the 1908 Gordon Bennett race are spilled onto a Berlin rooftop.

Crash-landed on a mountain, two German balloonists are about to fall to their death.

The drowning of a woman aeronaut in 1909 is dramatized in this magazine illustration.

said Eiloart, resembled "a ride in an elevator controlled by a mischievous child." On the fourth night the *Small World,* its ballast all but gone, ditched at sea after 1,200 miles. On a more familiar element, Eiloart, Mudie and crew sailed their 15-by-8-foot gondola-boat the remaining 1,500 miles to Barbados in 20 days. They suffered from a shortage of drinking water but otherwise came through the experience unscathed.

After the *Small World's* failure, more than a decade elapsed before any other balloonist felt confident enough to brave the Atlantic. Then a small rush of candidates appeared. Beginning in 1970, one aeronaut after another, at a rate of one attempt per year, took off from various points in North America with the hope of landing somewhere in Europe. Under this pressure, it seemed inevitable that the Atlantic must yield. But it did not; attempts to ride the high-altitude jet stream were unsuccessful, and at low altitudes, transatlantic balloonists were confronted by storms that consumed ballast and gas at such a rate that even the most skillful pilot could not make his resources last all the way across.

In an effort to solve the ballast problem, balloonists twice attempted the crossing with a helium balloon set inside a hot-air balloon; the idea was to regulate the buoyancy of the helium by surrounding it with temperature-controlled air. The concept was sound, but in practice these hybrids were unwieldy and neither balloon finished its journey.

Most aeronauts took their chances with simpler, helium-filled balloons. And chancy vehicles they were. Four men and one woman died in transatlantic attempts during the 1970s; others fell short after traveling distances ranging from a mere 20 feet—in the case of the aborted takeoff of a balloon piloted by magazine publisher Malcolm Forbes *(page 155)*—to the 2,740 miles covered in a 1976 attempt by Ed Yost.

Yost, father of the hot-air balloon resurgence of the 1960s, coaxed his aerostat *Silver Fox*—filled with helium—through good weather for 4½ days to a point only 700 miles short of Portugal. But there, gale-force winds threatened to bear him toward South America and he was forced to ditch, fortunately within sight of a ship that rescued him. Having nearly attained his goal—and in doing so breaking the distance and endurance records set by the Germans on their 1914 flight into Siberia—Yost might have been expected to try again. But when asked if he intended to do so, he replied with an unequivocal "No."

Yost never did try again, but he was to play an essential role in the expedition mounted by a team of American balloonists who had been inspired by his near-miss. No one read of the Yost voyage with greater interest than 42-year-old Max Anderson of Albuquerque, New Mexico. Anderson had become a millionaire from mining interests in uranium and other metals; he piloted his own airplane and was a charter member of Albuquerque's hot-air ballooning community. Yost had come so close to reaching the Continent that Anderson became convinced the feat was possible. The obvious risk involved in the journey did not deter him. As a younger man he had faced danger defending his mining claims in the desert, and as a balloonist he had been known to launch in

Arrayed in a field outside Liége, Belgium, nine entries from four nations await the start of the 1938 Gordon Bennett Cup race, which was won by a balloon from Poland. The next year, the Second World War forced cancellation of the contest and it was not resumed until 1979.

winds that were so strong they forced his envelope against the ground.

Anderson's friend and fellow aeronaut, Ben Abruzzo, had an even greater appetite for excitement under hazardous conditions. Abruzzo, the 47-year-old son of Sicilian immigrants, was a real estate developer who had built a ski resort in the mountains overlooking Albuquerque. Ben Abruzzo liked to fly. In his enthusiasm, he had cracked up in every type of aircraft he had tried except a helicopter, and he paid little attention to the bruises and broken bones he inevitably collected. Together, the men seemed a natural pair for the long-shot mission.

In mid-February of 1977, Anderson telephoned Abruzzo and put the question: "What would you think about you and me flying the Atlantic?" Abruzzo replied without hesitation, "Let's do it." The two men contacted Ed Yost; they considered him the only person in the United States who could construct a helium balloon capable of crossing the Atlantic. Yost agreed to build one for them. They had already decided that they would try the low-altitude route—less than 25,000 feet— rather than ride the jet stream at altitudes that would require a pressurized gondola. "We wanted to go in as pure a way as possible, in a romantic way," Abruzzo said later. "The more mechanical and sophisticated the flight was, the more outside involvement there would be, and the less satisfaction we could take in the end result."

Anderson and Abruzzo were well aware that they would have their hands full, between learning from Yost how to fly a helium balloon— neither man even had been in one before—and planning how best to take advantage of the winds over the Atlantic. They delegated most of the details of the flight to others. Yost, in addition to constructing the balloon, designed and built a gondola that was seaworthy, in case the crew had to ditch. Their friend W. C. "Doc" Wiley assumed the responsibility of equipping the gondola with radios, oxygen apparatus and the myriad other supplies needed for an anticipated five- to 10-day trip. He also saw that each item was labeled with its weight, so that the pilots would know its value as ballast.

To learn the meteorologic intricacies of the Atlantic, Anderson and Abruzzo turned to Robert B. Rice, chief meteorologist for an independent forecasting service. Rice, it pleased the aeronauts to discover, not only was on intimate terms with Atlantic weather but had a theory about how a balloon voyage across the Atlantic might succeed.

Rice explained that a cold front progresses across the ocean toward Europe in the form of a wedge, with a profile something like that of a doorstop. Above the slanting face of the wedge flow westerly air currents that could carry a balloon at speeds up to 60 miles per hour. If the aeronauts took off from the East Coast of the United States ahead of an approaching cold front and climbed above the advancing wedge, they could ride it across the ocean—or, as Rice capsulized his theory: "You can surf a balloon to Europe." There was one danger. The balloon had to remain above the wedge; if it did not, it would sink into thunderstorms below and behind the front and, if it survived these, would be drawn into cyclonic winds like those that had ended Ed Yost's attempt.

Both Anderson and Abruzzo instinctively felt that Rice had the answer they had been seeking. They hired him as their weather adviser, with the agreement that he would not discuss his theory with anyone else until after the flight; they wanted Rice's expertise for themselves.

On September 7, just the kind of cold front that Anderson and Abruzzo were waiting for began to forge across the United States. It would be upon them in 48 hours, and they scrambled to be ready in time. Much of their equipment was already positioned at a launch site not far from Boston. Ed Yost was summoned. He would install the all-important gas valve in the crown of the balloon, which they had christened *Double Eagle*—a name chosen for its echo of the Lone Eagle, Charles Lindbergh, as well as for its patriotic overtones. Yost would also supervise the inflation of the aerostat. But preparations lagged; a tool necessary for attaching the balloon to the gondola was mistakenly left in a distant workshop, causing a two-hour delay. And the storm front was approaching faster than expected; if the *Double Eagle* did not ascend ahead of it they might have to wait as long as a month for another one.

The pace grew frenzied. Finally, hours behind schedule but still ahead of the front, the *Double Eagle* ascended into the night, its gondola draped with necklaces of garlic, a Sicilian charm against evil spirits.

The $100 ride that became an obsession

American magazine publisher Malcolm Forbes discovered ballooning in 1972 through a newspaper advertisement that offered a ride for two people for $100. Never one to pass up an adventure, the 52-year-old Forbes made his first ascent a few mornings later, accompanied by his chauffeur. "One ride," Forbes said, "and I was hooked." The $100 whim became a multimillion-dollar passion.

In short order, Forbes added a Balloon Ascension Division to his family corporation (the chauffeur became its director); he bought a dozen hot-air balloons and converted one of his several residences—a splendid 17th Century castle in Normandy—into the world's first ballooning museum.

Forbes then set out to do things in a balloon that had never been done. In 1973, aided by a 30-member crew that followed in an airplane, a bus, several cars and a motor home, he became the first to cross the United States—with nightly stops—in a balloon.

Fourteen months later he invested one million dollars in the most ambitious balloon trip ever attempted: In an enclosed car supported by 13 helium balloons, he prepared to ride the jet stream nonstop from California, across the United States and the Atlantic, to Europe. But the balloons deployed prematurely, and Forbes barely escaped alive from the bouncing gondola; the Atlantic was left for others to conquer.

The picture of a modern aeronaut, Malcolm Forbes wears an all-weather flight suit and has a selection of protective helmets at his feet in this 1978 portrait.

The tardy takeoff proved to be only the first of the aeronauts' problems. Strong downdrafts over the Gaspé Peninsula in eastern Canada several times sucked the balloon toward earth—once to within 100 feet of the treetops—and forced the pilots to discharge more than a third of their ballast to remain airborne. Their timetable for climbing above the front having been disrupted by the turbulent air, they found themselves struggling through rain and snow. The balloon's envelope, instead of acting like a huge umbrella, actually funneled water past their ineffective rain shield and into the gondola, drenching the two pilots. To complicate matters, ice formed on the balloon, forcing it downward. Prodigious quantities of ballast had to be released to counteract the weight of the ice. Moreover, the southerly winds below 1,000 feet had carried them perilously northward toward Iceland and the Arctic Circle.

Cold had become a severe problem in the open gondola. Both men had rejected sailors' oilskins as superfluous; they had expected to ride high and dry, protected by the balloon. Anderson had chosen woolens that, even when damp, kept him adequately warm. But Abruzzo had opted for the goose-down gear he usually wore for skiing. Though the glossy clothing appeared waterproof, it was not; when the down became soaked, it lost all its insulating value. By the time the *Double Eagle*

Photographed by a remote-control camera during their successful crossing of the Atlantic in 1978, the crew of the Double Eagle II, Maxie Anderson (left), Larry Newman (foreground) and Ben Abruzzo, share their 17-by-6½-foot gondola with communications gear, three tons of ballast and a 30-day food supply. It was, in Anderson's words, "like living in a closet."

had been in the air 36 hours, Abruzzo was sure that he was freezing to death. Anderson could see his partner's distress and, though he felt certain they could still reach Europe if they simply climbed to a higher altitude, he radioed for a United States Air Force rescue helicopter, which set out immediately from Woodbridge, England. A few hours later, with the helicopter hovering nearby to pluck the pilots to safety, the *Double Eagle* ditched in 25-foot seas about three miles off the coast of Iceland. Once more, the Atlantic had prevailed.

"Within 24 hours after the end of the first flight," said Max Anderson, "I knew I was going to do it again." His main error, he thought, had been that he had not recognized the extent of Ben Abruzzo's physical distress until it was too late to help him. The next time, the pilots would have to communicate better, a difficult goal for these two individualists, who were highly competitive even when they were cooperating.

Initially, Abruzzo wanted no part of a second flight. His left foot had been severely frostbitten on the first attempt, and doctors warned him that even a mild recurrence would cost him his toes and perhaps the entire foot. But the foot mended over the next three months and Abruzzo found he could even ski comfortably if he wore heated boots. Gradually he changed his mind. "The fact that we almost made it," he remembered thinking, "said to me that we *had* to go again."

By early August 1978, *Double Eagle II* was poised for takeoff from Presque Isle, Maine, a starting point that would shorten the crossing by about 300 miles. The original gondola had been retrieved from the sea to be used again. Fitted with a more effective rain shield and rigged with a shelter containing a propane heater, the gondola would be significantly more comfortable. Wool clothing and oilskins, supplemented by parkas and sleeping bags lined with synthetic insulation that trapped heat even if it became wet, were chosen as the best ways to keep warm. As insurance for his foot, Abruzzo wore electrically heated socks.

The balloon itself was substantially larger than the earlier one. It had to be in order to lift the heaviest addition to the gondola: a third crew member. He was Larry Newman, 30 years old, a close friend of Abruzzo's who had been a skilled professional aviator before starting a hang-glider manufacturing company that had made him wealthy. Newman came accompanied by his favorite hang glider, which would be strapped under the gondola so that he could soar to a spectacular landing in France—if they made it that far.

Having a three-man crew would permit one to sleep and another to rest while the third stood watch. But it also raised the specter of one of ballooning's ancient hazards, the clash of inflated egos at close quarters in mid-flight. Anderson and Abruzzo had been a team for so long that their personalities—Abruzzo's energetic intensity and Anderson's cool detachment—had come to complement each other. The animated and exuberant Newman, whose ballooning experience was minimal, promised to alter the chemistry in the gondola.

The *Double Eagle II* would "surf" toward Europe ahead of a storm front, just as its predecessor had. (The accuracy of Bob Rice's weather strategy, which had become public knowledge after the 1977 flight, had been amply confirmed by an English-built aerostat, the *Zanussi*. Launched from Newfoundland ahead of an approaching cold front in July 1978, the *Zanussi* traveled almost the full distance before a rip in its helium envelope brought it down 100 miles from the French Coast.)

At Presque Isle on August 10 a new front was reported approaching. Just as before, there was a foul-up in preparing the *Double Eagle II* for getaway. The helium supplier, trying to save the balloonists money, sent only one truckload of the gas, less than had been ordered. As a result the inflation of the balloon, again supervised by Yost, proceeded so slowly that it could not be completed before the front arrived. The balloon had to take off only 85 per cent filled, a factor that would reduce its estimated endurance from a comfortable seven days to a barely adequate six.

Nearly three hours behind schedule, Abruzzo, Anderson and Newman took off just before 9 p.m. on August 11. The ascent began ominously; they had risen only 250 feet when wind currents on the lee side of a hillock plunged the balloon rapidly downward. As Newman's low-riding hang glider bounced along the ground, Abruzzo slashed a sandbag with his knife. Ballast streamed away, and the *Double Eagle II* began to climb toward the stars.

The balloon rose to 5,700 feet, its prescribed altitude for the night. By midday on August 12, as the sun warmed the helium, the balloonists expected to climb to 10,000 feet without further ballasting. Instead, the *Double Eagle II* hovered at 6,500 feet and remained at that altitude only because the crew released 65 pounds of ballast every hour, an extravagant but necessary expenditure if they were not to fall behind the front that was pushing them. Anderson suspected a leak as the cause of the balloon's sluggish performance; Abruzzo disagreed, arguing that a leaky balloon would have tended to sink during the preceding night rather than maintain its altitude as *Double Eagle II* had done. Nevertheless, Abruzzo scanned the dark interior of the envelope above with a flashlight, looking for a telltale star of light beaming through a hole. He saw nothing, but Anderson remained unconvinced.

On the second day out, the balloon behaved in the same way. Instead of rising in the noon sun, which was partly obscured by thin, high-altitude clouds, it sank—about 3,500 feet before Anderson's and Abruzzo's careful ballasting halted the descent. By the next day, however, the problem seemed to have corrected itself. The balloon rose to 15,000 feet and on the fourth day to 20,000 feet as the sun, unhindered now by high-altitude clouds, heated the helium. (Later it was concluded that so much of the balloon had been painted silver to reflect the sun that only full and unobscured sunlight would make it rise.)

The weather ahead of the ridge was perfect—dry and clear just as Bob Rice had promised. Larry Newman, when he was not asleep, talked almost incessantly, a characteristic that annoyed the two older

The Double Eagle II, eleven stories high, drifts majestically toward the end of its historic Atlantic crossing. "It's so quiet up there, so empty," said Anderson. "You move with the clouds like a particle of air."

crew members. He marveled aloud the first night at a shooting star he saw flashing across a shimmering curtain of northern lights. Another evening he tried and failed, between bites of a hot dog, to excite the others about a beautiful sunset. Abruzzo, irritated beyond his tolerance, snapped: "Larry, you're a goddamn babbling brook. Either talk less or say what you have to say in fewer words."

The reproach stung. Newman could not fathom why his companions were so taciturn. They had failed even to offer congratulations for what Newman considered his major triumph on the flight: fixing the gondola's balky radios, which had scarcely functioned for the first three days of the journey. As for Anderson, he had little to say to the third crew member except to suggest, early in the flight when he thought the balloon was seeping helium, that Newman lighten the gondola by soaring in his hang glider to a landing in Newfoundland.

Anderson repeated the suggestion on the fourth day out, as the *Double Eagle II,* short of ballast and traveling only about 20 miles per hour, approached the Shetland Islands. Gamely, Newman agreed to try, after extracting a pledge from Abruzzo and Anderson to tell the

A welcoming crowd swarms around the Double Eagle II after its landing in a wheat field near Miserey, France, on August 17, 1978. "It all went very well until the people got there," said crew member Ben Abruzzo. "We actually had to fight our way out of the crowd, and there was nothing left of the gondola or the balloon."

world of his sacrifice to the flight's success. Whether Newman would really have gone through with the hazardous leap became moot the next day as the balloon entered a new weather system that pushed it southeast toward Ireland at more than twice its former speed. It would be a close thing, but it looked as though all three of them would make it.

Later in the day, drifting in sunlit silence at 22,000 feet, the *Double Eagle II* suddenly began to fall at 400 feet per minute. Short of ballast, the crew could not afford to stop the plunge by throwing weight overboard; if they did so, the balloon might overreact and rise too high, venting so much helium in the ascent that they would not have enough ballast to keep them up when the gas cooled again at sunset. So they rode out the precipitous descent, expending as little ballast as possible as the balloon dropped past 10,000 feet and toward a layer of clouds below. No balloon had ever fallen so far so fast and remained in the sky.

But the *Double Eagle II,* gradually warming as it descended, slowed and then stopped in a large hole in the clouds, 4,000 feet above the ocean. Newman, pessimistically certain that the balloon would pass under the clouds where the sun could not heat it, bet Anderson $100 that they would not rise again. Moments later, however, the altimeter in

Exhausted but triumphant, transatlantic balloonists Anderson, Abruzzo and Newman respond to a crush of cameras. "What we've accomplished," said Anderson, "is not to make history, but to complete it. Ballooning started here in France in 1783, and since 1873 men have tried to fly the Atlantic. With good luck and good fortune, we've managed to finish that story."

the gondola registered a reassuring 6,500 feet. It dropped languidly back, then started to climb again, this time with more authority. As it passed 12,500 feet, a relieved Newman handed Anderson a $100 bill from his wallet. Together they watched in satisfaction as the *Double Eagle II* reached equilibrium at 25,000 feet and halted its ascent.

At sunset the three men jettisoned their extra food and water, their life raft, Newman's hang glider, even floor boards and interior bulkheads pried from the gondola—in order to maintain a safe altitude. And at 10:02 p.m. they crossed the Irish coastline. The aeronauts' reaction was strangely muted—no cheers, no elation. There were two reasons for this, as Abruzzo explained later: exhaustion and the strained relations among the crew. "Adrenalin," he said, "can overcome tiredness but not friction—that took the edge off the joy."

At dawn on August 17 the *Double Eagle II* was in sight of Wales. A squadron of small airplanes and helicopters materialized as they crossed Bristol Channel. It was the first hint of the jubilant public reaction to come. Over southern England, the aeronauts were dumfounded to see the morning sun sparkling from thousands of hand-held mirrors, signals of welcome from the people below. A message from the Smithsonian Institution in Washington was relayed by radio from London: Would the balloonists be willing to donate *Double Eagle II* to the Smithsonian? They replied that they would be honored.

Abruzzo desperately hoped to land in Paris, preferably at Le Bourget airfield where Lindbergh had touched down in 1927; the French, in anticipation of their arrival, closed the field to all other traffic. But the wind appeared to be bearing them south of the capital. A final argument erupted: Abruzzo wanted to try for Paris; Anderson and Newman favored landing sooner. Ultimately Abruzzo yielded to the majority. "What the hell," he said, "let's take her down and go sightseeing."

With 35 minutes of daylight remaining, they spotted fields planted in corn and barley next to a highway just outside the village of Miserey, 50 miles west of Paris. Planes and helicopters buzzed around the balloon as Abruzzo delicately valved helium, dropping the aerostat toward the hundreds of people who came swarming across the fields below. When the gondola thudded gently to earth, it dragged a short distance, driven by the wash from a press helicopter behind it. Abruzzo pulled the rip line. Seconds later they were engulfed by the mob.

Symbolically, the success of the *Double Eagle II's* flight was sublime: The climax of one of ballooning's finest achievements was at the same time a nostalgic return to its French birthplace. Nevertheless, Ben Abruzzo felt a momentary sadness. The great goal, finally achieved, now was gone forever.

Other goals remained, however. In May of 1980 Max Anderson and his son Kristian attained one of them, becoming the first to fly nonstop across North America in a balloon, the *Kitty Hawk*. The Atlantic Ocean had fallen but there was still the Pacific—and perhaps (dare one dream it!) even a balloon flight around the world. ～

A resurgent festival

Two inventions primed the resurgence of sport ballooning in the last decades of the 20th Century: a compact propane burner to keep the air inside the balloon hot, and a "rip-stop" nylon envelope that did not tear when punctured. New techniques, shown here in pictures by balloon photographer Vince Streano, replaced clumsy methods once used to inflate the gossamer giants. Large fans first filled a balloon with air, then propane burners heated the trapped air and kept it hot aloft, giving the balloonist better control over his altitude than ever before.

Thus equipped, the balloon once again became a catalyst of sociability. Sightseers drifted in them over game preserves in Africa and châteaus in France. Balloonists gathered by the dozens and hundreds at regional and national rallies and competed with contenders from other nations. The rallies drew crowds—like the 50,000 who came to the International Balloon Fiesta in Albuquerque, New Mexico, each October—that would have pleased even the proudest of their long line of predecessors, which began with Jacques Charles and the brothers Montgolfier.

After partly inflating the envelope with cold air from a large fan, an aeronaut uses a hose-fed propane torch to heat his 340,000-cubic-foot balloon, an unusually large size for sport ballooning.

A pilot checks the inside of his partly inflated balloon at the Hot Air Balloon Championships in Indianola, Iowa.

Transformed from amorphous masses of fabric, a multitude of balloons begins to rise at Albuquerque's 1979 International Fiesta, where 376 hot-air balloons were gathered.

An armada of aerostats fills the sky over
Albuquerque, whose clear skies and
interesting cross breezes at different altitudes
made it "the balloon capital of the world."

Acknowledgments

The index for this book was prepared by Gale Linck Partoyan. For their help in the preparation of this book, the editors wish to thank Paul Lengellé, artist *(endpaper),* Frederic Bigio, artist *(pages 56 and 126)* and Jerry Dadds, artist *(mailing-carton art).*

For their valuable help with the preparation of this volume, the editors wish to thank: **In Belgium:** Brussels—Albert Vandem Bemden, President, Belgian Aeronaut Federation; Albert Demuyter, Burgomaster; Madeleine Kipfer; Professor Georges Sylin, Brussels University. **In France:** Balleroy—Kassis Le Prieur, Curator, Château de Balleroy; Burcy—Jean-Michel Folon; Meudon—Audouin Dollfus; Paris—Cécile Coutin, Curator, Musée des Deux Guerres Mondiales; Hervé Cras, Director for Historical Studies, Musée de la Marine; Gérard Bashet, André Jammes, Éditions de l'Illustration; Gisèle Lambert; Jacques-Henri Lartigue; Bernard de Montgolfier, Curator, Musée Carnavalet; André Bénard, Odile Benoist, Elizabeth Caquot, Lucette Charpentier, Alain Degardin, Georges Delaleau, Gilbert Deloizy, Général Paul Dompnier, Deputy Director, Yvan Kayser, Général Pierre Lissarague, Director, Stéphane Nicolaou, Colonel Jean-Baptiste Reveilhac, Curator, Musée de l'Air. **In Great Britain:** Farnborough—Robert S. Lawrie, Alec Stenbridge, Royal Aircraft Establishment; London—Douglas Botting; J. S. Lucas, M. J. Willis, Department of Photographs, Imperial War Museum; Beryl Leigh, British Library; P. C. Timothy Marsh, City of London Police Museum; Michael Fitzgerald, Arnold Nayler, Royal Aeronautical Society; John Bagley, Martin Andrewartha, National Aeronautical Collection, Wendy Sheridan, Pictorial Collection, Science Museum; R. Williams, Department of Prints and Drawings, British Museum; Marjorie Willis, BBC Hulton Picture Library. **In Italy:** Milan—Sandro Taragni; Rome—Dr. Marco Malavasi; Countess Maria Fede Caproni, Countess Timina Caproni Guasti, Museo Aeronautico Caproni di Taliedo. **In Japan:** Osaka—Osamu Asai, Asai Collection; Tokyo—Akio Fujii, Susumu Naoi, Shinkichi Natori, Tadashi Nazawa, Katsuko Yamazaki; Yokohama—Kanagawa Prefectual Museum. **In The Netherlands:** Amsterdam—Martin de Vries; The Hague—Mrs. J. Boesman. **In Spain:** Captain Enrique Alvarez Novo; Captain Ramón Hidalgo Salazar. **In Switzerland:** Basel—Dr. Eugen Dientschi; Lausanne—Jacques Piccard. **In the United States:** Colorado—Donald Barrett, Duane Reed, Air Force Academy Library; Diane Johnson, National Center for Atmospheric Research; Delaware—Daniel Muir, Curator, Pictorial Collections, Eleutherian Mills Historical Library; Washington, D.C.—Phil Edwards, Mary Pavlovich, Dominick Pisano, Mimi Scharf, Catherine Scott, Pete Suthard, National Air and Space Museum; Dr. Russell Parkinson; Massachusetts—Harvard Theatre Collection, Harvard University; Larry Salmon, Museum of Fine Arts; Helen Slotkin, Institute Archives and Special Collections, M.I.T. Archives; Minnesota—Jean Nelson; New York City—Paul Blum; Janet Byrne, Curator, Department of Prints and Photographs, Julia Meech-Pekard, Associate Curator, Department of Far Eastern Studies, The Metropolitan Museum of Art; Virginia—Dana Bell, U.S. Air Force Photo Depository. **In West Germany:** Augsburg—Alfred Eckert; Hamburg—Dr. Bernhard Heitmann, Museum für Kunst und Gewerbe; Munich—Rudolf Heinrich, Johann Romalo, Herbert Studtrucker, Deutsches Museum; Münster—Dr. Siegfried Kessemeier, Westfälisches Landesmuseum; Bernard Korzus, Antonia Mertens, Westfälisches Museumsamt; West Berlin—Dr. Roland Klemig, Heidi Klein, Bildarchiv Preussischer Kulturbesitz.

The editors also wish to thank Janny Hovinga, Wibo van de Linde, Amsterdam; Bob Gilmore, Auckland; John Burgess, Bangkok; Enid Farmer, Boston; Brigid Grauman, Brussels; Nina Lindley, Buenos Aires; Frank Sleeper, Cape Elizabeth, Maine; Sandy Jacobi, Copenhagen; Rick Stoff, Fenton, Missouri; Alex des Fontaines, Otto Gobius, Robert Kroon, Geneva; Bing Wong, Hong Kong; Peter Hawthorne, William McWhirter, Johannesburg; Martha de la Cal, Lisbon; Michael Hapgood, London; Diane Asselin, Los Angeles; Jane Walker, Madrid; Felix Rosenthal, Moscow; Dag Christensen, Oslo; Sara Day, Philadelphia; Sherly Uhl, Pittsburgh; Mary Johnson, Stockholm; Peter Allen, Sydney; Traudl Lessing, Vienna; Bogdan Turek, Warsaw.

Bibliography

Books

Adler, Irene, *Ballooning: High and Wild.* Troll Associates, 1976.

Amick, M., *History of Donaldson's Balloon Ascensions.* Cincinnati News Company, 1875.

Andrée, S. A., Nils Strindberg and K. Fraenkel, *Andrée's Story: The Complete Record of His Polar Flight, 1897.* The Viking Press, 1930.

Bacon, John M.:
The Dominion of the Air: The Story of Aerial Navigation. Cassell and Company, Limited, 1902.
By Land and Sky. London: Sir Isaac Pitman and Sons, Ltd., 1908.

Baldwin, Munson, *With Brass and Gas: An Illustrated and Embellished Chronicle of Ballooning in Mid-Nineteenth Century America.* Beacon Press, 1967.

Blanchard, Jean Pierre:
Journal and Certificates on the Fourth Voyage of M. Blanchard. London: Baker and Galabin, 1794.
The First Air Voyage in America. Reprint. Penn Mutual Life Insurance Company, 1943.

Blanchard and Baker, *The Principles, History & Use of Air-Balloons.* C. C. Van Alen, 1796.

Block, Eugene B., *Above the Civil War: The Story of Thaddeus Lowe, Balloonist, Inventor, Railway Builder.* Howell-North Books, 1966.

Brewer, Griffith:
Ballooning and Its Application to Kite-Balloons. London: Air League of the British Empire, 1940.
Theory of Ballooning. Government Printing Office, 1918.

Butler, Frank Hedges:
Fifty Years of Travel by Land, Water and Air. London: T. F. Unwin Ltd., 1921.
5,000 Miles in a Balloon. London: H. Cox, 1907.

Cavallo, Tiberius, *The History and Practice of Aerostation.* London, 1785.

Chandler, Charles deForest, *How Our Army Grew Wings: Airmen and Aircraft Before 1914.* The Ronald Press Company, 1926.

Cornish, Joseph Jenkins, III, *The Air Arm of the Confederacy, A History of Origins and Usages of War Balloons by the Southern Armies During the American Civil War.* Official Publication #11, Richmond Civil War Centennial Committee, 1963.

Cottrell, Leonard, *Up in a Balloon.* S. G. Phillips, 1970.

Coxwell, Henry, *My Life and Balloon Experiences.* London: W. H. Allen & Co., 1889.

DeFonvielle, Wilfrid, *Adventures in the Air.* London: Edward Stanford, 1877.

De Nansouty, Max, *Aérostation.* Paris: Paris Ancienne Librairie Furne Boivin et Cie., 1911.

Diehl, Walter S., *Balloon and Airship Gases.* The Ronald Press Company, 1926.

Dollfus, Charles, *The Orion Book of Balloons.* Orion Press, 1961.

Dollfus, Charles, and Henri Bouché, *Histoire de L'Aéronautique.* Paris: L'Illustration, 1942.

Drattell, Alan, and Jeanne O'Neill, *Journey to Deptford.* Deptford Township, N.J., 1976.

Dwiggins, Don, *Riders of the Winds: The Story of Ballooning.* Hawthorn Books, Inc., 1973.

Ege, Lennart, *Balloons and Airships.* Macmillan Publishing Co., Inc., 1974.

Emme, Eugene M., *Aeronautics and Astronautics: An American Chronology of Science and Technology in the Exploration of Space 1915-1960.* National Aeronautics and Space Administration, 1961.

Emme, Eugene M., ed., *Two Hundred Years of Flight in America: A Bicentennial Survey.* Univelt, Inc., 1977.

Faujas de Saint-Fond, Barthélemy, *Descrizione delle esperienze della macchina aerostatica.* Venezia: Stamperia Graziosi, 1784.

Fergusson, Sir James, *Balloon Tytler.* London: Faber and Faber, Ltd., 1972.

Fisher, John, *Airlift 1870: The Balloon and Pigeon

Post in the Siege of Paris. London: Max Parrish, 1965.

Forster, T., Annals of Some Remarkable Aerial and Alpine Voyages. London: Keating and Brown, 1832.

Full Particulars of the Greatest Aerial Voyage on Record from St. Louis, Mo. to Adams, New York in Nineteen Hours: Experience of the Travellers. A. Donnelly, 1859.

Garrison, Paul, The Encyclopedia of Hot Air Balloons, Drake Publishers, Inc., 1978.

Gibbs-Smith, C. H., Ballooning. London: Penguin Books, 1948.

Giffard, Henry, Le Grand Ballon Captif à Vapeur. Paris: G. Masson, Éditeur, 1878.

Glaisher, James, ed., Travels in the Air. London: Richard Bentley, 1871.

Haddock, John A., Mr. Haddock's narrative of his hazardous and exciting voyage in the balloon Atlantic with Prof. Jno. LaMountain. Haddock & Sons, 1873.

Haining, Peter, The Dream Machines. London: New English Library, 1972.

Haydon, F. Stansbury, Aeronautics in the Union and Confederate Armies, Vol. 1. The Johns Hopkins Press, 1941.

Hildebrandt, A., Balloons and Airships. Yorkshire, England: EP Publishing Limited, 1973.

Hodges, Goderic, Memoirs of an Old Balloonatic. London: William Kimber, 1972.

Hodgson, J. E., The History of Aeronautics in Great Britain. Oxford: Oxford University Press, 1924.

Hoehling, Mary, Thaddeus Lowe: America's One-Man Air Corps. Kingston House, 1958.

Honour, Alan, Ten Miles High, Two Miles Deep: The Adventures of the Piccards. Whittlesey House, 1957.

Jeffries, Doctor, A Narrative of the Two Aerial Voyages of Doctor Jeffries with Mons. Blanchard; with Meterological Observations and Remarks. London: J. Robson, 1786.

Jomard, Conté. Paris: E Thunot et Cie., 1852.

LaChambre, Henri, and Alexis Machuron, Andrée and His Balloon. Westminster, England: Archibald Constable & Co., 1898.

Lunardi, Vincenzo, Mr. Lunardi's account of his ascension and aerial voyage. London, 1785.

McCarry, Charles, Double Eagle. Little, Brown, 1979.

Magoun, F. Alexander, and Eric Hodgins, A History of Aircraft. McGraw-Hill, 1931.

Marion, F., Wonderful Balloon Ascents: or, the Conquest of the Skies. Scribner, Armstrong, and Co., 1874.

Mason, Francis K., and Martin C. Windrow, Air Facts and Feats: A Record of Aerospace Achievement. Doubleday & Company, Inc., 1970.

Mason, Monck, Aeronautica; The Theory and Practice of Aerostation. London: F. C. Westley, 1838.

Mikesh, Robert C., Japan's World War II Balloon Bomb Attacks on North America. Smithsonian Institution Press, 1973.

Milbank, Jeremiah, Jr., The First Century of Flight in America. Princeton University Press, 1943.

Monk, F. V., and H. T. Winter, Adventure Above the Clouds. London: Blackie & Son Limited, 1975.

Norgaard, Erik, The Book of Balloons. Crown Publishers, 1971.

Parkinson, Russell Jay, Politics, Patents and Planes: Military Aeronautics in the United States 1863-1907. University Microfilms, Inc., 1963.

Partington, J. R., A History of Chemistry, Vol. 3. London: Macmillan & Co., Ltd., 1962.

Philp, Chas. G., The Conquest of the Stratosphere. London: Sir Isaac Pitman & Sons, Ltd., 1937.

Piccard, Auguste:
Between Earth and Sky. London: Falcon Press, 1950.
In Balloon and Bathyscaphe. London: Cassell and Company, Ltd., 1956.

Pilatre de Rozier, François, La vie et les mémoires de Pilatre de Rozier, écrits par lui-même, 1786. Paris.

Pineau, Roger, Ballooning, 1782-1972. Smithsonian Institution Press, 1972.

Poe, Edgar Allan, The Complete Tales and Poems of Edgar Allan Poe. Vintage Books, 1975.

Poole, Lynn, Ballooning in the Space Age. McGraw-Hill, 1958.

Porter, Harold E., Aerial Observation. Harper and Brothers, 1921.

Rhees, William Jones, Reminiscences of Ballooning in the Civil War. Meadville, Pa., 1898.

Rolt, L. T. C., The Aeronauts: A History of Ballooning, 1783-1903. Walker and Company, 1966.

The Romance of Ballooning: The Story of the Early Aeronauts. A Studio Book, The Viking Press, 1971.

Rotch, Abbott Lawrence:
Benjamin Franklin and the First Balloons. The Davis Press, 1907.
Sounding the Ocean of Air. London: Society for Promoting Christian Knowledge, 1900.

Scrivner, John H., The Military Use of Balloons and Dirigibles in the United States, 1793-1963. Norman, Okla., 1963.

Simons, David G., Man High. Doubleday & Co., 1960.

Smith, Anthony, Jambo, African Balloon Safari. E. P. Dutton, 1963.

Stehling, Kurt R., and William Beller, Skyhooks. Doubleday & Co., 1962.

Tissandier, Gaston:
Le grand ballon captif à vapeur de m. Henry Giffard. Paris: G. Masson, 1879.
Histoire des balloons et des aéronautes célèbres. Paris: H. Launette & Cie., 1887-1890.

Turnor, Hatton, Astra Castra: Experiments and Adventures in the Atmosphere. London: Chapman and Hall, 1865.

United States Naval Aviation, 1910-1970. Department of the Navy, 1970.

Upson, Ralph H., Free and Captive Balloons. The Ronald Press Company, 1926.

Wilkinson, Stephen Frank, Lighter Than Air. London: Arthur H. Stockwell, Ltd., 1939.

Wise, John:
A System of Aeronautics. Joseph A. Speel, 1850.
Through the Air. Arno Press, 1972.

Wykeham, Peter, Santos-Dumont: A Study in Obsession. Harcourt, Brace & World, Inc., 1962.

Periodicals

Abruzzo, Ben R., M. Anderson and L. Newman, "Double Eagle II Leaps the Atlantic." National Geographic, December 1978.

"Ballooning." Abercrombie and Fitch Co. Catalogue, 1912.

Bassett, Preston R., "Aerial Adventures of Carlotta, The Lady Aeronaut." American Heritage, August 1966.

Boesman, Jan, "Gordon Bennett Balloon Race." The Hague: Catalogue of The Netherlands Aeronautical Museum, 1976.

Brown, Dick and Donna, "A Broken Date With The Jetstream." Ballooning, Spring 1975.

Cohen, Bernard I., "Benjamin Franklin and Aeronautics." Journal of the Franklin Institute, August 1941.

Cooper, Mabel C., "An Early Bird Goes to Paris." U.S. Air Services, September 1931.

Dime, Eric A., "America's First Aeronaut." Air Travel, January 1918.

Douty, Esther M., "The Greatest Balloon Voyage Ever Made." American Heritage, June 1955.

Eiloart, Arnold, "Braving the Atlantic by Balloon." National Geographic, July 1959.

"First Atlantic Crossing." Time, August 28, 1978.

"Flight of the Eagle." Newsweek, August 23, 1978.

Gammon, Clive, "Across the Sea to Glory." Sports Illustrated, August 28, 1978.

Harrison, George H., "Taking Off." Natural Wildlife, June-July 1975.

Jares, Joe, "A Bunch of Basket Cases." Ballooning, June 11, 1979.

Kittinger, Joseph W., and Volkmar Wentzel, "The Long, Lonely Leap." National Geographic, December 1960.

Lahm, F. P., "The Memories of a Pioneer." Flying, August 1957.

Lewis, Richard Warren, "Exotic Adventurers, A Sky Full of Hot Air Balloons." California Living, Los Angeles Herald Examiner, March 25, 1979.

National Air and Space Museum, Smithsonian Institution, biographical files:
Howard, James T., "30 Years in the Air." New York World-Telegram.
Lahm, F. P., "Ballooning and Aerial Navigation."

"National Geographic Society-U.S. Army Air Corps Stratosphere Flight of 1934 in the Balloon 'Explorer,' " National Geographic Society Contributed Technical Papers, 1935.

"National Geographic Society-U.S. Army Air Corps Stratosphere Flight of 1935 in the Balloon 'Explorer II,' " National Geographic Society Contributed Technical Papers, 1936.

Nordheimer, Jon, "Balloon Accident Blocks Ocean Trip." The New York Times, January 7, 1975.

Palmer, Henry R., Jr., "Lighter-Than-Air Flight in America, 1784-1910." Journal of American Aviation Historical Society, Fall 1979.

Sackett, Barbara, "Albuquerque International Balloon Fiesta—1978." Ballooning, November-December 1978.

Salmon, Larry, "Ballooning: Accessories After the Fact." Dress: The Journal of the Costume Society of America, Vol. 2, No. 1, 1976.

Sherard, Robert M., "Gaston Tissandier, the Balloonist." McClure's Magazine, May 1895.

Stevens, Albert W., Capt., "Man's Farthest Aloft." National Geographic, January 1936.

Wellman, Walter, "Long-Distance Balloon Racing." McClure's Magazine, July 1901.

"The Whole World to See." Time, August 28, 1978.

Picture credits

Index

Printed in U.S.A.